KW

PATTY SHEEHAN ON GOLF

PATTY SHEEHAN ON GOLF

**PATTY SHEEHAN
AND BETTY HICKS**

TAYLOR PUBLISHING COMPANY
DALLAS, TEXAS

Published by Taylor Publishing Company
1550 West Mockingbird Lane
Dallas, Texas 75235

Designed by Hespenheide Design

Library of Congress Cataloging-in-Publication Data
Sheehan, Patty, 1945–
        Patty Sheehan on golf / Patty Sheehan and Betty Hicks.
            p.   cm.
        Includes index.
        ISBN 0-87833-910-8
        1. Sheehan, Patty, 1945–   . 2. Golfers—United
States—Biography.   3. Golf for women.   I. Hicks, Betty.   II.
Title.
GV964.S49A3   1996
796.352'092—dc20   95-53051
[B]   CIP

Printed in the United States of America
10   9   8   7   6   5   4   3   2   1

This book has been printed on acid-free recycled paper.

CONTENTS

PREFACE

Edgar Jones, head golf professional of Reno, Nevada's, Hidden Valley Country Club, introduced Patty and I in 1971. She was a sturdily-built 13-year-old Hidden Valley junior golf star. As a member of the Wilson Sporting Goods Company's Advisory Staff, I was at Hidden Valley to present a golf clinic and to play nine holes with Ed Jones. "Betty," Ed said on the practice tee as I was warming up for my clinic, "I'd like you to meet Patty Sheehan."

I recognized immediately that the kid possessed the consummate motivation, the "B.D." as Betsy Rawls and I called it, borrowing a phrase from former Notre Dame football coach Frank Leahy. The burning desire. The B.D. is the foundation upon which an athlete's achievements are built. This 13-year-old girl had the B.D.; she exuded it.

Thus, I was not surprised as I stepped into the grand ballroom of Reno's Hilton Hotel on November 13, 1993, to attend with 500 other friends and fans of Patty Sheehan her induction into the LPGA Hall of Fame.

The influences, the events, the inspirations, the traumatic disappointments that Patricia Leslie Sheehan experienced between 1971 and 1993 are described in *Patty Sheehan on Golf.*

Patty Sheehan on Golf began its life as *Rain Delays and Rainbows*, the latter title being most descriptive of the frustrations of weather delays on the LPGA tour and of Patty's optimism, which is best reflected in her maxim, "Rainbows always follow rain delays." But few golfers would understand the nuances of that title, so Patty's treatise on the game of golf was given a more golf-descriptive title.

Patty Sheehan on Golf also started out to be an autobiography. But we had not written many chapters until I became aware of the crippling restriction imposed by the autobiographical approach. Not only is Patty reluctant to praise herself, she is equally reluctant to say anything derogatory about anyone else. So the book became part authorized biography, giving its writer free reign within the constraints of truth and decency. But as the title promises, when Patty Sheehan talks golf, the words are hers, including all of chapter one and the tips, wisdom, and musings that follow chapters two through eight. In these sections Patty discusses, in her own words, what she thinks, what she feels when she is swinging a golf club, when she is reading a green, when she is playing in a competition.

Patty's approach to the golf swing, conveyed to her by PGA teaching professional Ed Jones, may be considered unique in this era of high-tech analysis, of golf stars who create golf books based on exotic methodologies or upon dissecting a golf swing into innumerable mechanical components. "I can't play that way," Patty Sheehan says bluntly. "I can't play by mechanics. I play by feel." And then she discusses what she means by *feel* and how she has acquired it. Her teacher laughingly claims that any

book he would write on the golf swing would contain about three pages; Ed Jones is adamant about keeping the golf swing the simple motion it truly is. Patty Sheehan shares the secrets of that simple motion with you on these pages. She also shares the revelations of what made her the Hall of Famer she is today, and why she has been awarded numerous formal accolades for her humanitarianism, so rare in today's world of self-centered, greedy athletes.

Massive project that *Patty Sheehan on Golf* was, sorting out the super-abundance of material concerning one of the greatest women athletes of the 20th century, the chore was a rewarding one, because the revelations about Patty Sheehan's life reinforced a tenuously-held hope that star athlete and exemplary human being are not contradictory terms.

—Betty Hicks

CHAPTER ONE

BUILDING THE CLASSIC SWING

Mary Bryan, ESPN's golf commentator, is my next-door neighbor in Palm Springs, California, so Mary might be accused of subjectivity when she said into her microphone at one LPGA tournament, "If there is any swing on the LPGA tour you should copy, it's Patty Sheehan's. Her swing is classic."

What's classic? Beethoven's Fifth? The Mona Lisa? Michelangelo's *David*? My definition of "classic" is the following: any creation which stands up to the test of time because it does not deviate from the standards of perfection for a particular art form. Classic golf swings are rare.

I like to think my swing is classic because that's how a guy named Edgar Jones taught it to me. Ed got to work with all those athletic genes I inherited from Leslie and Bobo Sheehan, my mom and dad. In my childhood I showed off my athleticism on the ski slopes. I was a champion at that sport, too, when I

was a kid. Through skiing I learned the fundamentals of balance so important to a golf swing. Add to the formula the competitive motivations my brothers, Butch, Jack, and Steve, instilled in me in my childhood and you've got a great combination for a tournament golfer. Maybe even an LPGA Hall of Famer.

But it's my golf swing on center stage here. Did Ed Jones really start out by saying, "I'm going to teach Patty the classic swing?" No, he did not. And can an 18-handicapper who plays golf once or twice a week and who hates to practice develop a swing like mine, or even learn from my golf swing? Yes, definitely. Can the man who has been my professional teacher since I first enrolled in his kids' classes at Reno's Hidden Valley Country Club at age eleven reveal the fundamentals and philosophies of swing he applied to my development? Another affirmative! Can Ed

1

I swing my driver. The limitation of still photographs of a golf swing, however classic that swing may be, is that stills cannot reveal the rhythm of the swing. Another limitation is that the player may be tempted to mentally caption each photograph, leading her to believe that she should be thinking at each position of the swing. I play by feel, not by thinking of mechanics. I can point out that I allow my body to follow the force I produce in the clubhead. Note that I let my left heel come off the ground on the backswing (5). My teacher, Ed Jones, agrees with famed Harvey Penick that allowing the left heel to come off the ground helps the player achieve control at the top of the backswing. Notice, too, that while my left arm is comfortably extended on the backswing, it is not stiff (5).

© Cheryl Traendly

1

2

5

6

9

I want to point out some features of the swing that might contradict alleged fundamentals your self-appointed professional might have said were essential in the swing. My left arm is only comfortable at the top of the backswing; it is definitely not straight (4). The left arm is straight at impact, however, but that's because of the centrifugal force produced in the clubhead; the arm extends automatically (6). No way do I think of that! It should be apparent I let my left heel come well off the ground, permitting my body to turn (4). But I do not *think* to turn my body!

3

4

7

8

The worst advice in golf is "Keep your head down." You cannot fix your head rigidly after impact and create a free-moving follow-through. Notice (7) that my head is permitted to rotate into the finish. Actually, my head moves slightly back on the downswing, as you'll see if you align my head the small bush in the background. Do I do that consciously, and should you? I answer that with a loud "No!"

All players have what I call mannerisms, simply a different way of making a particular move. One of my mannerisms is letting my right toe slide in the direc-

tion of my left foot on the downswing. Notice my stance is more narrow at the finish than at the top of the backswing (8). Once again, I do not do this consciously, nor would I recommend that you incorporate the move into your swing. Ben Hogan made that same move, but I doubt he would attribute his success to that right toe slide.

©Cheryl Traendly

Jones' concepts produce results for golfers who are not talented athletes and for whom golf is not a top priority? Of course they can.

Ed Jones believes in a sound grip, good balance, compactness in the swing. Ed Jones also believes that a golfer can only think of one thing at a time.

Betty Hicks once wrote in *Golf for Women* magazine, "There's nothing about those concepts that will burn any holes in the ozone layer. They're what are known as 'The Fundamentals.' But embracing the fundamentals promises no more reward than endorsing the work ethic, mom and apple pie, and the sack race at the company picnic.

"Golfers shop for the same kind of gimmickry and promises and oratory that made the flock converge on Jim Jones in Guyana. Like headache sufferers clawing at drugstore shelves, they're looking for anything other than fundamentals.

Fundamentals: translation: "You gotta work at it, you must make

I have Ed Jones check my swing occasionally, just to make sure I'm not picking up any bad habits. You, too, might consider taking preventive golf lessons, rather than waiting until you have "grooved" an error for six or eight months before you ask a golf professional to repair it, magically, in thirty minutes.
© *Cheryl Traendly*

some uncomfortable changes, and you may temporarily give up a few strokes in your transition."

Grip. Balance. Compactness. One correction at a time. That is how Eddie Jones worked with me to build the classic swing. Ed Jones says today, "I can't honestly say when I met Patty that I said to myself, 'Oh, boy! Here's a winner!' It's difficult, working with kids, because club grips are always too big for them. They just can't grip the club right to begin with."

My memories of meeting Ed are vivid, because he was drowning in a sea of kids. All of my ski buddies played golf in the summer, so I played with them. (We needed to fill the competitive void left when the ski season ended.) I was not a pretty sight as a golfer. I was frustrated by the game. I hated it. I was not patient, and I had serious problems in my swing.

I've never outgrown my frustrations, but my hatred of the game has lessened significantly. That Ed and I worked out my serious swing problems is a fact that is now a part of golf history.

LESSON 1. THE TRAUMA OF HOLDING THE CLUB

I had just played in the All-Teens Tournament in Reno, sponsored by

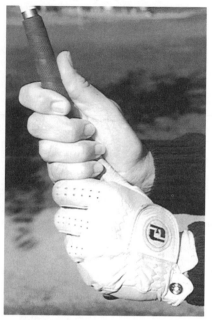

A ten-finger grip is sometimes erroneously called the "baseball grip." You wouldn't grip a baseball bat that way! In a ten-finger grip, correctly called "the unlap grip," you simply do not overlap your hands. It's a great grip for kids and anyone with small or weak hands.
© Cheryl Traendly

a genuine nice-guy optometrist, Dr. Don Zunini. I was eleven years old, not even a teen, but they let me into the tournament because they didn't have enough girls entered. I thought I was pretty hot stuff, the spikes of my first golf shoes clattering on the asphalt walkway at the country club.

Then one day George Archer—the same George Archer who stars on the PGA senior tour now—stopped by where I was practicing. George was working on his golf swing with Ed Jones back then.

"You'll never be any good," George told me, sensing, I think, that I wanted to be good, "until you give up that ten-finger, hook grip."

A ten-finger grip is sometimes called the baseball grip in error. You wouldn't grip a baseball bat that way. In a ten-finger grip, you don't overlap. There's nothing wrong with a ten-finger grip. But most good players use the overlapping grip, sometimes called the Vardon grip because the famous British professional, Harry Vardon, who had enormous hands, started overlapping to keep all of his fingers on the club's gripping surface. Just because a high percentage of good players use the overlapping doesn't automatically make it the best grip, because probably 99 percent of golfers who can't break 100 use it, too.

Ed Jones says that for a golf club to have a handle small enough for a kid to grip, you'd have to peel the grip material off down to the bare metal. So I had a kid's grip on the golf club when George Archer saw me.

Changing that grip was my first trauma in golf. I worked and worked to get it right. Grip changes

If you have already learned to hold the club, check to make sure your grip is correct. Take your grip and set the club-head on the ground in front of you. Unfold your palms from the shaft. The underside of the shaft should now be resting across the center of your fingers or close to the center. If the underside of the shaft lies on your palms, you have a problem with your grip that will affect your swing.
© Cheryl Traendly

are the worst changes a golfer has to make. But George's "you'll never be any good" ate at me. There was just no way I wasn't going to be a good golfer, as tough as that grip change was for me.

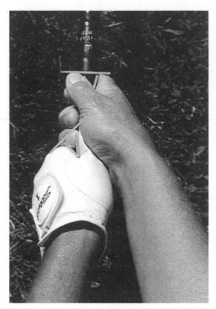

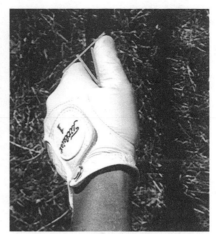

Looking down at the left hand grip from the player's perspective:
The V formed by the inner sides of the thumb and forefinger is pointing to the right shoulder. The thumb and the forefinger are about the same distance down the shaft.
© Cheryl Traendly

Two more methods of checking the correctness of your grip involve asking yourself a couple of simple questions:
1. Are my thumb and forefinger of each hand about the same distance down the shaft?
2. Are the Vs in each hand pointing toward my right shoulder?
© Cheryl Traendly

LESSON 2. TECHNIQUES OF HOLDING THE GOLF CLUB

If you are already a golfer, I'll show you how to check to determine if you hold the club effectively. (I really prefer the word "hold" to "grip." "Grip" implies tension.)

If you are a beginning golfer, it's best for you to learn how to hold the club with the assistance of a

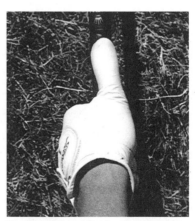

The "long thumb" grip. The thumb is significantly farther down the shaft than the forefinger. There's a hazard of damaging your hand with the long thumb.
© Cheryl Traendly

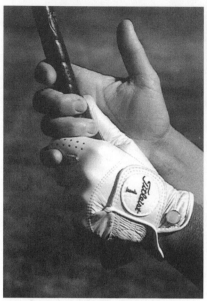 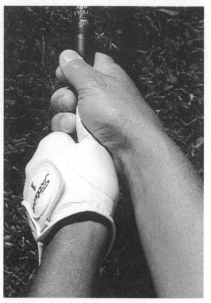

Obviously, amputating your thumb would be a drastic cure for the long thumb. Instead, use the trigger grip. Allow the shaft to lie across the knuckle of the forefinger on each hand as if you are squeezing a trigger on the shaft's underside.

© Cheryl Traendly

Another view from the player's perspective. This grip—mine—meets the criteria for a good hold on the club. If I opened my hands, the underside of the club shaft would lie in my fingers. My thumb and forefinger are close to an equal distance down the shaft, and my Vs in each hand point to my right shoulder.

© Cheryl Traendly

teaching professional, because pitfalls are numerous and need to be corrected on sight.

But to check your already established hold on the club, take your grip with the clubhead resting on the ground. Unfold your palms from the shaft. The underside of the club shaft should now be resting across the center of your fingers. If the underside of the shaft lies back toward the base of the fingers, or even into your palms, the problems with your grip will invade your swing.

There are two more checks for gripping efficiency. With your hands placed on the club in holding position ask yourself this: Are my thumb and forefinger in each hand approximately the same distance down the shaft? If your thumb is farther down the shaft in either hand, that's the "long thumb" position. Though some teaching professionals advocate the long thumb, they're not paying your doctor bills. You *could* hurt yourself with the long thumb by bending a tendon or two. If either thumb is significantly farther down the shaft than its respective forefinger, you'll need to correct long thumb by gripping with the underside of the shaft more toward the tip knuckle of the forefinger. Mickey Wright called the forefinger the "trigger finger," because its position is like squeezing a trigger on a gun.

You can also use those nebulous Vs in either hand to critique your grip. I use the word "nebulous" because many golfers do not know what forms the Vs or where to look for them. The Vs are formed by the small gap between the thumb and forefinger in each hand, at the point in the grip where they cease being adjacent. The Vs should, in the case of an average right-handed golfer, each point to the right shoulder.

Ed Jones says, "I talk a lot about the Vs to people. And I make sure my students don't slip into the long thumb position."

I'm sorry to say I rarely see a high-handicap golfer—and I play with a lot of them in pro-ams—who has a good hold on the golf club.

A sensitive subject involving grip is those high-fashion, talon-like nails that are so popular with women. At the risk of inviting the wrath of some very stylish ladies, I need to say bluntly, "You can't grip a golf club right with those fingernails."And I don't care if they do make special peekaboo gloves now that accommodate the nails. The nails are still there, peekin' through the fingers of the gloves, trying without success to find a way to fit into your grip without gouging the palms of your hands.

LESSON 3. HOW TO IMPROVE YOUR GRIP WITHOUT ACTUALLY CHANGING IT

To repeat: grip changes are the worst corrections to make in the game of golf. Changing a grip is very uncomfortable, and that discomfort disrupts your swing pattern.

So, before you change your grip, check to determine if your club grips need changing first. Ed Jones says, "At least 75 percent of my students' clubs I pull out of their bags on the lesson tee need to have grips replaced. I'm not trying to sell them a new set of clubs. I'm just advising them there's an advantage they're not capitalizing on. Compared to a new set, new grips are a very minor expense."

Caution: be sure to buy the size that fits your finger length! Grip size is not based upon an inexperienced shop assistant muttering, "Aha, a man—men's grips," or "Aha, a woman—ladies' grips." Grip size is not based upon your height or your weight or your sex. The size of your grip is tailored to the length of the center finger of your right hand. On a piece of paper, trace that finger from base to tip, *including* the *normal* length of the nail, either homegrown or acrylic. Measure the length in inches and in fractions. The grip installer will then use a table of measurements to determine the correct diameter of your new grips.

Just because the wrong-size golf grips don't pinch—unlike ill-fitting shoes—doesn't mean grip size is not as important as shoe size in making your equipment fit you.

The problem is you won't notice your grips are approaching slickness. Slickness happens gradually. I change my club grips every three months. My caddie, Carl Laib, is responsible for monitoring their condition. Compare your grips with a new set in your favorite golf shop to determine if they're slick. Or have your golf professional decide for you. Then replace them!

LESSON 4. BALANCE

Balance throughout the swing is established at address position.

When I was eleven, my good balance surprised Ed Jones, although that was about the only aspect of my golf techniques that made Ed smile. By the time I started golf lessons with Ed, I had already skied competitively for seven years. Yeah, you have it right. I had skied competitively since I was four year old.

Ed has observed that most skiers—and he has had a lot of skier-golf students in Reno—stand back on their heels. For some reason, I never had that problem.

It should be obvious that Ed considers the advice golfers sometimes received to stand back on their heels a problem, not a solution.

Stand erect, with your heels about shoulder width apart, toes turned slightly outward. Keep your knees straight for the moment. Bend just enough from your hips (*not* from your waist) so that when your arms hang easily from your shoulders, there is about six to eight inches between your legs and your arms. Keep your upper spine as straight as possible, and as Ed says, "Stick your butt out." I do, distinctly. You'll notice that this position moves your weight toward your toes. Now flex both knees forward.

The address position—"pounce" position. Balance throughout the swing is established at the address position, so you must be attentive to every uncomfortable, awkward-feeling detail of it.
© Cheryl Traendly

A method of measurement to evaluate your knee flexion is to place a club shaft beside your right heel and your right hip. Open your right hand to a full hand span. There should be a hand span of flex between the front of your knee and the club shaft.

Take a moment to observe what happened to your weight distribution. About evenly distributed, isn't it, between the balls of your feet and your heels? That's good because you can't hit the ball effectively from your heels and you can't hit it effectively when your weight is on your toes.

To fine tune your stance, bend your knees in toward one another as though you are holding a large softball between them. Now your weight concentration has moved slightly to the inside of each foot—pounce position.

Once you have established good balance at address, let balance-in-motion just *happen* as you swing. That is, don't attempt to force balance to occur. Ed says, "I'm simple-minded. All my instruction revolves around the theme of simplicity. If you're balanced at address, *let* your body move with your swing and you'll probably stay balanced throughout the swing, as long as your right leg is stabilized."

We'll talk about the right leg later. You lefties will unfortunately have to do your own reversals throughout this book, as it's cumbersome writing "right or left" or "back foot/front foot" or however else we phrase both sides of the golf swing.

To initiate the stance, or address position, I stand erect, with my heels about
shoulder width apart, toes turned slightly outward. Notice I have my hands
slightly ahead (or to the left) of the ball.
© Cheryl Traendly

I bend just enough from my hips so that
when I allow my arms to hang from my
shoulders there is about six to eight
inches between my legs and arms. My
knees are slightly bent. I have heeded
Ed's admonition to "Stick my butt out."
My upper spine is as straight as possible, compatible with extending my arms
slightly toward the ball. What are all
these flexings and staightenings and
sticking-outs about? They're about correct weight distribution, which happens
automatically as you assume your
stance.
© Cheryl Traendly

Here I have bent my knees in slightly toward one another, as though I were holding a large softball between them. This causes my weight automatically to shift toward the insides of my feet.
© *Cheryl Traendly*

LESSON 5. THE SWING

Let's play a word association game. You're watching my golf swing on a television infomercial, on Sybervision, or on an LPGA telecast. Describe my swing in one word. Good for you. You said "Compact!"

Ed Jones has led a lifelong crusade to eliminate wasted motions in his students' golf swings. With a big assist from those athletic genes I own, plus my skiing experience, Eddie sure succeeded with me. My swing is compact.

When I say "compact," I mean free of unnecessary motion. No parts of me are flying when I swing a golf club. Nowhere does the club move out of its natural plane, the angle through which I swing.

Ed could remind you that while I am a natural athlete, I was not a natural golfer when I started the game. Maybe great athletes are not automatic classic swingers of the golf club because a golf swing is an unnatural motion.

I can laugh now at the kid golfer I was. I was not a pretty sight. I overswung, and I had a loop and a reverse weight shift. But Ed and I worked with some gimmicky things. Gimmicky? That's golf slang for a teaching aid. "Gimmick" isn't necessarily derogatory, although some people use the word with a negative connotation if they don't agree with the technique the aid is trying to teach. I'm endorsing a line of teaching aids on television as *Patty Sheehan on Golf* goes to press. I have used all of these aids in more primitive forms at some time in my career. You'll be seeing them throughout this book. I assure you they'll help with movement problems in your swing.

Among the gimmick things that Ed used with me was Mickey Wright's doorstop under the outside of my right foot. One element of balance that can be helped at address position is keeping the weight on the inside of the right foot and the right knee bent at the top of the backswing.

I also endorse the arm band that appears in the Natural Swing Products swing package, promoted by a group of golf-addict investors in Denver, Colorado. There's very little original or innovative in golf instruction. Someone else has usually invented a teaching aid in a primitive form decades ago. One of Mickey Wright's first professional teachers, Harry Pressler, used the arm band when teaching Mickey. I've heard that a pro named Abe Mitchell used the arm band even before Harry Pressler did.

The arm band is actually a slight variation on the handkerchief Ed Jones once put under my right arm to keep that arm from flailing— "chicken winging," it's called—on the backswing.

The Swing Singer came from Mickey Wright's first pro, Johnny Bellante. Bellante cut a small branch off a nearby eucalyptus tree, handed it to Mickey and said, "Mickey, I want you to make this branch sing." So Mickey swung the branch until it sang. Probably when Johnny was little, another pro cut a branch for him and told him to make it sing. What we're talking about here is maximum acceleration through the ball. Because you may not live near a eucalyptus tree, the Swing Singer was scientifically designed to accomplish the same goal.

The most important factor in applying any of the many of so-called "fundamentals of swing" is that you avoid paralysis by analysis. This is essential when you start golf and as you progress from one level to the next in the game. The important question is this: How many things can you think about in the less than two seconds required to swing a golf club?

I play golf primarily by feel. I don't play by mechanics. All that "slow back, wrists cock midway on the backswing, left arm straight, club square at the top, weight shifted 85 percent to the right foot at the top, downswing started by a pull of the left arm and a shift of the weight to the left foot, wrists remain cocked until midway down, finish low and around"—that stuff's not for me! You simply cannot think too much and still swing a golf club. I think one of the reasons golfers have trouble with concentration is that they can't zero in on a single thought; they have too much to think about. And the books, magazines, and videos are all guilty of contributing to the confusion.

LESSON 6. SWING DRILLS

In learning to swing, you can't go wrong adhering to Ed Jones' principles of balance, sound grip, and swing simplicity. So, keep it simple by swinging to waltz music! You can't go wrong with "The Beautiful Blue Danube." You may make mistakes by overdoing a swing technique, but you can't overdo trying to achieve certain fundamentals. And you cannot overdo swinging to waltz time.

The Swing Singer. Use the Swing Singer to hear the "eucalyptus branch" sing. Then you'll know you are really swinging the clubhead,

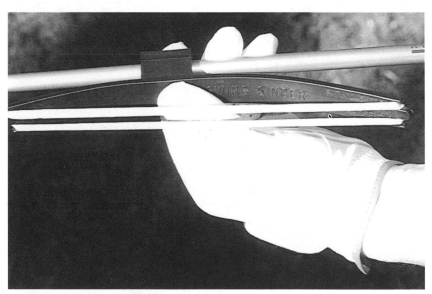

A golfer clamps the Swing Singer onto a club shaft. Mickey Wright's first teacher cut a eucalyptus branch off a tree and told her, "I want you to make this branch sing!" The Swing Singer was engineered by a physicist to sing—and loudly!—when a golfer swings it. If a player can make the Singer sing (actually, it's a one-toned vibrating sound) he or she is truly swinging the club.
© Cheryl Traendly

rather than lifting it, shoving it, pulling on it. Practice a few swings with the Singer. Then hit ten or twelve practice balls, trying to duplicate that same swinging action.

The Stabilator. Use the Stabilator, the foot wedge, to achieve balance throughout your swing. Take a few practice swings with the Stabilator in place. Then hit a few balls with the Stabilator bracing your right foot and leg. Take the Stabilator off. Now try to get the same feeling the Stabilator gave you as you swing at practice balls.

The Impassifier. Drill for a few swings with an arm band on. The Natural Swing Products arm band is adjustable to all sizes and is called the Impassifier because the famed teacher, the late Ernest Jones,

The Stabilator. Mickey Wright used a doorstop under the outside of her right foot. The Stabilator has been modernized by Natural Swing Products, Inc., and made more suited to its specific purpose—to keep the weight on the inside of a player's right foot, which enables a golfer more readily to keep the right knee bent. The Velcro strap/fastener allows the player to move about the practice tee with The Stabilator in place.
Photo by Betty Hicks

Patty demonstrates the Impassifier.
© Cheryl Traendly

The Signature Expander. Application of the Expander to the swing is described below.

© Cheryl Tracndly

warned his students, "Swing the clubhead with your hands and let the arms and shoulders look on impassively."

The Signature Expander. Use the Signature Expander for a few successive swings. Then transfer that same feeling of the clubhead swing to your swing with the club by itself. Hold the Expander with its cord held on your club. Make some continuous half swings, making sure you are truly swinging so the Expander is swinging in synchronization with your clubhead. Ernest Jones was known for his jacknife on the end of a bandana to demonstrate a swinging motion. But the people at Natural Swing Products didn't want you bopping yourself on the head with a jacknife, so we substituted softer material in our Expander.

Combining the aids in your drills will make a meaningful practice session, but take it easy. Don't try to use all of the aids at the same time. You may combine, for example, the Impassifier and the Stabilator. Or swing the Swing Singer with the Impassifier in place. Or use each aid separately in your practice session. To know which aid you need to concentrate on most, have your golf professional with you on the practice tee.

The next task is probably the toughest: to transfer the feel you experienced using the swing aids from the practice tee to your swings on the golf course.

PATTY SHEEHAN TALKS PUTTING

The number of how-to words written on a golf technique seems to be in direct proportion to the amount of frustration caused by that part of the game. That's possibly why there have been more valueless or even harmful words written on putting than on any other part of the game. Putting's frustration quotient is very high.

The technique of putting is loaded with worthless warnings. "Never up, never in." That's the one I hate the most. The late Helen Dettweiler, a pioneer LPGA professional, paraphrased that advice with "Always up, never in." I feel the same way about it. Even with a

right line, a ball hit with enough momentum to go six feet past the hole is going *over* the hole, not *into* the hole.

Then there's "relax!" Now, honestly, how do you tell someone to relax when that person is paralyzed by the fear of missing the putt she's facing?

"Anchor your elbows to your hips." In my book, that's nothing but another way to push and pull putts.

Is there any putting advice that works? Yes, there are tips that help me do what I consider most important about putting: get that thing in the hole as fast as I can! But I didn't get these tips from studying other golfers. I got one tip off television. I got another from my experience as a junior skiing champion working with my dad, a onetime Olympic ski team coach. (I know that sounds strange because golf and skiing don't seem connected.) And I got a lot out of reading *Harvey Penick's Little Red Book*.

I know that's a strange combination of sources, but I'll explain.

A tip Ken Venturi gave on a television show helped me a lot. He said, "Keep the butt end of the putter moving toward the hole as you stroke through the ball." That's been very successful for me because it helps me keep my left elbow away

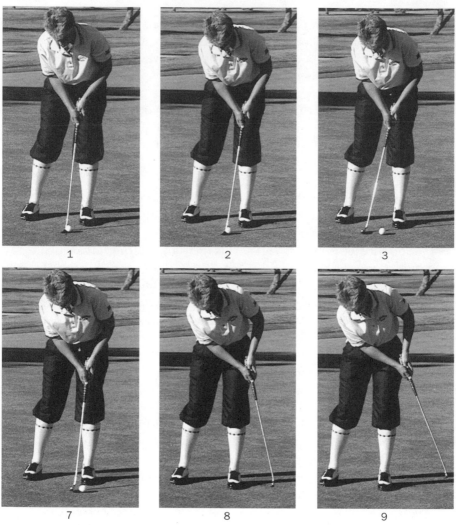

1   2   3

7   8   9

I use a standard address position for putting: weight on the left foot, ball opposite the left heel, hands opposite the left leg, eyes over the ball. Grip: reverse overlapping. But my initial move is distinctive. Note that my hands have moved from position opposite my left inner thigh (1) to opposite the center of my left leg (2). This is a *forward press*. The purpose of the forward press is to overcome the inertia—the stagnant status of the club at address—with a slight motion of its own, sort of like a baseball pitcher's windup. There are not many LPGA tourists who exploit the advantages of the forward press in putting. The backswing begins with a small movement of the arms and shoulders. Notice that the angle between the hands, wrists, and arms is changed very little from the original address position. The

clubface is square—at right angles to the line of putt. The clubface continues square to the line of putt (3–9). The relationship between the hands, wrists, and arms continues constant through the follow-through. Here I demonstrate the principle I learned on television from Ken Venturi's commentary: Keep the butt end of the putter moving toward the hole on the follow-through. Another putting fundamental I show emphatically here is to keep the follow-through the same length as the backswing (5 and 9). This principle avoids the error of decelerating on the downswing, a devastating mistake in putting.

© Cheryl Traendly

EDGAR MILTON JONES

Edgar Milton Jones is a seventy-two-year-old native of Ravenna, Ohio. A graduate of Ravenna High School, he briefly enrolled at Ohio Wesleyan University. But in 1943 Uncle Sam beckoned. Ed Jones enlisted in the Army Air Corps. Following flight training, Ed became the commander of a lumbering, four-engine B-24 "Liberator" bomber, famed for its heroic role in the Ploesti oil field raids that helped change the face of World War II in favor of the Allies.

Edgar Jones returned from the war unscathed, despite twenty missions over Europe. The veteran faced two obvious choices: return to college or become an airline pilot. Instead, he followed his heart into the game that hooked him in his boyhood: golf. Edgar Jones became a golf professional in 1948.

After varied club professional apprenticeships, Ed Jones took his golf skills on the PGA tour in 1958. But his game was a thin level below that demanded of touring pros. So in August of 1958, he settled into the position of head professional at the Hidden Valley Country Club, a private facility nestled in eastern foothills of Reno, Nevada. Twenty-four years later, he retired from his full-time work and began to teach part-time. Every Monday he climbs on the club tractor and mows the driving range.

At Hidden Valley, Ed wore the many hats club professionals necessarily don: tournament director, golf equipment merchandiser, club psychologist, social arbiter, and golf teacher. In the latter role, he met a sturdily built eleven-year-old junior ski champion, daughter of Hidden Valley members Bobo and Leslie Sheehan. Her name was Patricia Leslie Sheehan. "Just call me Patty," the kid told Ed Jones.

from my body. This is important, because the left arm acts as a leader in keeping the club on line.

The skiing connection is about a theory known as the "fall line." Translated, that's the point-to-point direct way down the hill. If you rolled a ball down a mountain, it would automatically follow gravity, wouldn't it?

You may have heard teaching professionals say recently, "All putts are straight." Well, obviously putts are not always straight because they follow gravity and they break. The point is that when you've figured out the break on a putt, you putt straight for the spot to the right or left of the cup, disregarding the cup. Then just let the fall line take it from there.

You may have noticed, watching me in person or on television, that unlike most of the LPGA players, I never have my caddie help me line up putts. Why, when some of these golfers have the caddie do everything but hit the ball for them? Because even ol' know-everything Carl doesn't know where on the putter I'm going to hit the ball. My caddie can't know how hard I'm going to hit it. Both these factors directly influence the amount of break the putt will have. That means, of course, that if I misread it, I have to blame myself, not my caddie!

I have the most trouble reading bermuda greens in flat states, like Florida, because I have trouble figuring which way is west. On bermuda greens, the grain—which way the grass is growing—is a fac-

tor we don't have to be too concerned about on today's verticut bent grass greens. You might have read in Penick's *Little Red Book* about Ben Hogan asking the caddie, "Which way is west?" A non sequitur? Not according to my horticulturist acquaintances, who tell me that like other plants, grass grows toward the light. The tendency is called phototropism, so if you can figure out which way is west, you can factor that into your green reading.

You may have seen cartoons of golfers equipped with an assortment of meteorological instruments—wind gauges, thermometers, barometers, and hygrometers. The cartoon is supposed to be funny because using all of this paraphernalia to read a three-foot putt is obvious overkill. And now we need to add a magnetic compass to all that other equipment!

You can get too technical about a simple but frustrating golf technique. As the great Ernest Jones used to say, "Just because golf is elusive is no reason to complicate it." That thought is the foundation of my whole approach to putting.

CHAPTER TWO

THICK, RICH AND STEAMING HOT

For Leslie Sheehan, professor of nursing at Porter Hospital in Middlebury, Vermont, it was to be a vacation nonpareil. Leslie's destination: Cortina, Italy, site of the 1956 Winter Olympic games. Her husband, Bobo, father of her three young sons and a Middlebury College athletic coach, was also the coach of the United States Olympic ski team.

Leslie recalls, "When I knew Bobo was going to Cortina in December, I decided this was my big chance to go to Europe. I talked my friend, Lee Myhre, into going with me. Then I did everything I could to earn extra money. I took in sewing, worked as a school nurse, and worked in a hospital operating room." These chores were in addition to Leslie's regular position as a nursing professor.

So Leslie and friend Lee bought tickets to Italy and joined the winter Olympians. Bobo begged a liberty pass from the Olympic village for an evening and made the most of it.

Was it an omen that Patty Sheehan was conceived at the Winter Olympics in 1956? Did the circumstances of her conception predestine Patty to become a junior ski champion and then turn her athletic abilities toward becoming an LPGA Hall of Fame golf champion?

Did Leslie and Bobo Sheehan want another boy? "Heck no!" Leslie exclaims. "I wanted *six* boys when I got married—and then I *had* two." Then there were three—Robert Jr. (Butch), John (Jack), and Stephen (Steve)—and then there was Patricia Leslie (Patty).

Bobo remembers, "We almost named her Cortina."

Patty had a storybook, normal childhood in a storybook, normal family. The currently popular phrase "family values" could well have been coined by the Sheehans.

Barry McDermott, writing in *Sports Illustrated* magazine in the early 1980s, said, "Happiness was something Sheehan never had to search for while she was growing up in Middlebury. If the Sheehans were soup, they would be thick, rich and steaming hot, the kind that sticks to your ribs."

Bobo Sheehan and Marion Leslie Ireland met in high school in Newport, Vermont, in 1943. Leslie's brother Bob went with Bobo's sister Rae.

Bobo's father had a bread route. His mother made doughnuts. "God! Were they good!" Leslie recalls. "Just plain ol' doughnuts. The house smelled like doughnuts. I loved dates with Bobo! Bobo smelled like doughnuts."

Patty's scrapbook of clippings announces that "Miss Marion Leslie Ireland, daughter of headmaster and Mrs. Elwood R. Ireland of Gould Academy, became the bride of Robert Richard Sheehan, son of Mrs. G. Ray Sheehan of Newport, Vermont on June 14, 1947. The bride," reported the newspaper, "was a graduate of the University of New Hampshire and the Yale University School of Nursing. For the year before being wedded to Robert 'Bobo' Sheehan, she had been an instructor in Medical Sciences at the New England Baptist Hospital in Boston. Mr. Sheehan [Bobo] is a graduate of Middlebury College and served with the Naval Air Force."

My, how he served! Robert was a dive-bomber pilot flying SBD Dauntless and the SB2C torpedo bomber aircraft off two carriers. Three-foot putts to win the money never bothered Bobo after pointing the noses of his bombers at the hulls of warships and pulling out of screaming dives surf-high at six Gs. "No real exciting adventures," reports the taciturn pilot, who logged about 600 hours during the war in the Pacific.

Patty Sheehan's entry to the world was announced over the loudspeaker system at a Middlebury College football game her father was coaching. The speaker blared, "Here's a final: Patricia Leslie Sheehan, seven pounds, fifteen ounces." The date was October 27, 1956.

"Everyone in the stands who knew Mom and Dad cheered louder for me than they did during the game. I think the roar stuck in my brain, because the hospital was right across the street from the football field."

Patricia was exposed to golf when she was still a toddler. Leslie and Bobo were both golfers, but on a college coach's salary, the Sheehans couldn't afford a baby-sitter, so they'd plop Patty down on Mother's pull cart and off they'd go. Once in a while they'd let four-year-old Patty swing at a ball with the 2-iron Bobo cut down for her. But the game frustrated her.

"I was always crying and throwing fits." Though the crying and fits were long gone thirty-four years later, golf evoked similar emotions. "Is there any game as rewarding and yet as frustrating?" Patty would ask in 1993 upon her induction into the LPGA Hall of Fame.

When Patty was big enough—about six or eight, she'd guess—she began caddying for her mother—for twenty-five cents a round. Leslie remembers there were a lot of "oh, Mothers" when Patty was caddying for her. But Leslie did break 100 three times that first summer with her new bag toter, in spite of the frequency of the "oh, Mothers."

"I remember she pulled my golf cart when I played in the 1966 state amateur in Burlington. I shot a 42–57–99. I can still see her face on the front nine, as it was my lowest nine-hole score ever. She was so proud of me."

"No Hall of Fame for Mom," says Patty. "I can't remember her as ever carrying anything but an 18-handicap." But Leslie Sheehan loved to play golf, Hall of Fame or not.

Twenty-five cents became an important number in Patty's early golf. That's exactly what Dud Phinney at the Middlebury Golf Club charged for junior golf lessons. She began taking lessons from Dud when she was four—and has con-

tinued to thank Dud for her first exposure to the discipline demanded by golf.

"Dud taught us how not to kill each other in junior class." Beginning golfers, especially kids, have no concept of the extent of a swing arc. "And he made us responsible for the balls we hit. Dud made a game of picking up our practice balls. That was really more fun than hitting them. He also taught us to be responsible for paying for our lessons."

Patty literally began skiing as soon as she could walk. A brief entry in her scrapbook notes that the Sheehans entered her in the Lollipop Race in Middlebury when she was four. Patty skied like a kid possessed to get to the finish line and win a strawberry-flavored lollipop. "We had some eight millimeter movies of me skiing when I was real little. Boy, I went down that hill like a bat out of hell! You couldn't even see my legs!"

Patty confesses now, "I was the rottenest little kid on the ski slope. I'd cut in front of people in the lift line. I'd ski under people's legs. My brothers' girl friends used to tell me how bad I was. I'd get a friendly slap on the butt once in a while, just so I knew who was boss."

Since Bobo coached many Olympic skiers, Patty spent her

childhood chasing Olympians downhill. A former Middlebury College ski team member, John Morton, remembered the prodigy well. He wrote for Upper Windsor's Vermont public radio his vivid recollections of Patricia Leslie Sheehan:

> *Bobo Sheehan was the legendary ski coach at Middlebury College from just after World War II until 1967. Under his guidance, Middlebury ski teams consistently finished well in the NCAA Championships and provided plenty of skiers to our Winter Olympic teams.*
>
> *Middlebury is blessed with its own ski area, located high on the spine of the Green Mountains between Ripton and Hancock. The focal point of the Snow Bowl used to be the intimidating fifty-meter ski jump which reached high up the mountain side. The hill record on Middlebury's jump was more than 200 feet, and even a terrified beginner could sail well past 100 feet.*
>
> *From the top, the base lodge at the end of the outrun seemed to be miles away. The takeoff was ten feet high, constructed of logs backfilled with earth. The landing hill seemed as wide as a football field, and was so steep*
> *that we had to cling to a rope as we side-stepped down to pack it after a snowfall.*
>
> *In those days Middlebury College was overrun with excellent alpine racers, but a good team performance on the collegiate circuit demanded top finishes in jumping and cross-country as well as slalom and downhill. So, many of us with marginal alpine skills volunteered to ski cross-country and also to jump. Cross-country racing was hard work, but jumping could be terrifying, especially on icy or windy days.*
>
> *For several of us, ski jumping wasn't really a sport; it was a question of survival. We tried to keep our knees from visibly knocking as we sped down the inrun. We never actually jumped; we simply coasted over the takeoff, arms flapping like frantic seagulls. Any time we made it from the landing hill to the outrun standing, it was a jump worth celebrating.*
>
> *Into this world of college men, bravely facing the dangers of speed, flight, and the harsh winter elements, entered the coach's nine-year-old daughter. Little Patty Sheehan trudged up the stairs of the Middlebury ski jump with her tiny alpine skis*

over her shoulder. She had long since conquered every downhill trail on the mountain.

As she reached the knoll where her dad stood coaching his college jumpers, she announced that she was going to give it a try.

"Why don't you ride the landing hill first," Bobo suggested.

"Naw, I wanna take it from the top," she answered brightly, as she filed in among the college skiers headed up the trestle.

At the top of a big ski jump, the tension can get pretty thick. There isn't a lot of small talk; people are pretty focused. When they finally get in the starting chute, it's not uncommon for an athlete to double-check his bindings or his goggles three or four times out of pure nervousness.

Patty didn't know any of this. She chatted cheerfully with the serious college jumpers, until she noticed the guy in the chute check his bindings for the sixth time.

"Cheez, are you gonna check your bindings all afternoon, or are you gonna jump?" she asked with a mixture of impatience and youthful innocence. Embarrassed, the college jumper stepped aside and said to the nine-year-old, "Well, if you're in such a big rush, be my guest."

As an answer, she wrinkled her nose at him, grabbed the railing, and launched herself down the inrun. She held her downhill tuck through the air, disappeared over the knoll, and seconds later emerged as a tiny dot headed toward the base lodge.

Thereafter, any time the jump was packed out, you could be pretty sure Patty would be riding it on her little alpine skis, laughing and joking with the college jumpers.

It's no surprise to me that Patty Sheehan is one of the best on the LPGA tour. I saw her poise, self-confidence, and athletic ability when she was a nine-year-old ski jumper."

The geographical coincidence of Patty Sheehan's conception was not alone in destining her to be an athlete; heredity had a major role. Bobo was a star in football, baseball, and skiing. Leslie played all kinds of sports to the limit then allowed to "ladies." Patty's paternal grandfather, Ray Sheehan, was a talented baseball player. "The genes go way back," explains Bobo. "I knew she was an athlete when she was four, watching her keep up with her older brothers. She was a better football player than any of the boys."

Patty remembers her earliest athletic thrill. "During halftime at a Middlebury College football game, a bunch of us kids—I guess I might have been about eight—went out on the field for an informal exhibition game," recalls sports historian Patricia. "Real tackle, we played. I was the only girl playing.

"Well, I caught a pass and ran it in for a touchdown, fighting off would-be tacklers all the way. How that crowd cheered! I loved it. I'd never been in front of a bunch of people and heard them applaud—especially applaud me. The cheers sent little chills up and down my spine. My throat got lumpy. Swallowing was hard. Thirty years later I still like doing things that make people cheer—like knocking irons stiff, getting up and down from bunkers, and draining forty-footers."

Patty Sheehan, with no apologies, admits she grew up a tomboy. Cultural attitudes have changed; it seems to be okay to grow up a tomboy these days. Sociological studies have found that tomboys develop leadership qualities, such as resourcefulness, assertiveness, independence, that assure success when they become ex-tomboys.

"Yeah, I grew up a tomboy. What's my definition of tomboy? All your friends are boys. You play football, baseball, basketball, run track, do field events. Not playing with dolls. Hanging out with your older brothers. Having fun. Getting into mischief. That's what being a tomboy means."

Leslie remembers, "Patty was always better in everything than the other kids. She was a leading scorer in basketball, in spite of being only five foot, three inches. I knew she could have been an Olympic skier. She'd just stick that little chin out and go for it." Bobo added on behalf of the young Sheehan males, "All the kids were wonderful skiers, but they never did anything with it."

"Anything" is a father's modest evaluation. Butch was on the Junior National Ski Team. Jack was United States Junior Ski Champion. Steve was a ski team star. But the Sheehan brothers did not limit their athletic exploits to skiing. Butch was a football standout. He played to scratch in golf and is now a teaching professional in Nevada, where he was once state golf champion. Jack was an all-state football player and an interscholastic track champion in the pole vault. Sister Patty says admiringly, "I've never seen a better pole vaulter than Jack." Steve also starred in football, was a great skier, a scratch golfer, and interscholastic golf champion in both California and Nevada.

Patty Sheehan had three great golf swings to mimic.

The Sheehan offspring were lucky to have access to college facilities—real trampolines, for example, on which they could train. "Hey, let's go to the gym!" was preface to a Sheehan stampede.

The four siblings were also the "golf course architects" for "Sheehan Country Club" that encircled their Middlebury farmhouse. A pole vault pit was their sand bunker. The swimming pool that the four guys (Bobo, Butch, Jack, and Steve) and Patty, then six, dug in the backyard was their water hazard. At one point they considered making a "hole" based on hitting over the three-story house. Luckily for the Sheehan windows, they nixed that one.

They had a dirt floor in the garage in which they dug holes for cups during their winter rounds. Patty observes, "I think the Stimp* reading must have been about a twenty! Maybe that's where I devel-oped my putting touch—on that greased lightning garage floor."

In 1967 Bobo was offered a position as vice-president and general manager at California's Alpine Meadows Ski Resort. At forty-five years old, both of Patty's parents wanted to move. "We were in a midlife crisis," says Leslie. "If we were going to make a career change, then was the time. By then Bobo had been at Middlebury College for over twenty years." Bobo took the position at Alpine and the family, with only Jack dragging his heels, pulled up their Middlebury stakes and moved west. Jack left his heart in Vermont; he was to return shortly when he was fifteen. "He missed his high school sports and his girl friend, who he later married," explained Patty.

"A Major Blow to the State of Vermont" mourned the headline in the *Vermont Sunday News* of May 21, 1967. "It will be a major setback," wrote sports scribe John Canvelis, "losing this great coach and gentleman from the Vermont sports scene.

"And, it will be a tremendous blow if Bobo and Leslie Sheehan's

---

* A Stimpmeter is a simple mechanical device which measures the speed of a green. It is graduated on a scale of one to twenty. Twenty on a Stimpmeter is very, very fast, faster even than Augusta National for the Masters, faster than any USGA Open course.

kids—Butch, Jack, Steve and Patty—outstanding young athletes all—leave the state of Vermont."

Alpine Meadows is near Lake Tahoe, so the Sheehans lived for a year in the scenic splendor of the Sierras. Patty was eleven when the family moved to Reno in 1968 and opened Bobo Sheehan's Ski Shop.

Leslie Sheehan confesses to having two lifelong ambitions: to chair a school of nursing and to own a ski shop. She achieved both goals in 1968 in Reno. And she was doing both jobs simultaneously.

With her ivy-draped master's degree in nursing from Yale University, Leslie was a prize acquisition for the newly founded School of Nursing at the University of Nevada in Reno. Leslie's innovative program included cooperative television teaching between the campuses in Reno and Las Vegas. She explained, "I taught some classes to my students that were televised to UNLV and their instructors taught classes that were telecast up to my students." Leslie also supervised the student nurses' clinical work at local hospitals.

Two years later the Western Nevada Community College, a two-year institution, opened and Leslie won the privilege of creating their nursing curriculum, hiring instructors, setting up the laboratory, and direct-

ing the program for three years. "After work at the college, I would change uniforms and my patients became customers at the ski shop."

The nursing program grew rapidly, and nursing professor-ski shop proprietor's duties became overwhelming. It was priorities time. "So I made the decision to become a shop owner only." From 1974 to 1986 Leslie confined her workday efforts to her role as bookkeeper, clerk, buyer, and seamstress in charge of ski clothing repairs. At day's end she tended to her brood of four, until 1975 when the boys had all achieved their independence and the brood dwindled to one—Patty.

Patty considered Bobo Sheehan's Ski Shop her second home. Early in the ski shop's existence, Patty would bus to junior high school, complete her numerous after-school activities, then go to the ski shop and thence home with Leslie and Bobo. "She loved to make sales and write up sales slips," Leslie recalls.

The youngest of the Sheehans continued in competitive skiing, but out west, it was a whole new ball game. "The meets were unorganized compared to those in the East," Patty commented. "The races weren't run on time. The snow was not as hard packed as in Vermont.

We even had to boot pack [pack the snow by tromping on it in ski boots] the run before we could race. Even though I was number one in the country in my age group by the time I was thirteen I felt quittin' time coming on."

During the summer the junior skiers of Reno all played golf. Most played at Hidden Valley Country Club. The Sheehans had joined Hidden Valley before they moved downhill from the Tahoe area. Later they bought a house near the club, an inadvertent act of foresightedness that placed Patty close to PGA golf professional Edgar Milton Jones.

Next to her father, the most important man in Patty Sheehan's life has been Ed Jones, Hidden Valley's head golf professional from 1958 until his retirement in 1982. "He was on the practice tee giving little kids lessons when I met him. I decided I'd better get into Ed's junior program. I'm still in it, twenty-eight years later! That is, I'm still working on my game with Ed." Except for Butch, Jack, and Steve, who give Patty a tip now and then, Patty has never had any teacher other than Edgar Jones.

"As a young golfer I was not a pretty sight." Patty grins. "I had only one club—the 2-iron I'd used for every shot since I was four. I had serious problems in my swing.

"So I *hated golf!* Golf is an extremely difficult game to learn, especially for kids with their short attention spans. But my family all played. So it was either play or be left home alone. I played. I think that if we had stayed in Vermont, I would have stuck with skiing. But I stumbled into something pretty big for myself in golf. And I stumbled into the 'pretty big' part very young."

There was a golfer-optometrist in Reno named Dr. Don Zunini. Every year he sponsored the All-Teens Tournament at Hidden Valley.

Patty indulges in a brief soliloquy. "Let me see," she says to herself. "Eleven doesn't end in a teen. Twelve doesn't end in a teen. Not until I blow out thirteen candles on my cake will I be a teenager."

At age eleven, Patty bemoaned the reality that she would have to wait two years to play in the tournament. Then a little bit of Irish luck; the tournament didn't have enough girls entered, so they let Patty play in spite of her age.

"Boy, did I *love* that competition! Playing in a tournament gave me a really, really good feeling, like I was walking on golf spikes that were a foot long. Dr. Zunini's tournament was the real beginning of my relationship with the game of golf. It gave me the push I needed, because I *hated* losing."

Patty won the All-Teen Tournament the following year, when she was twelve. "We got to pick our prizes. The girl who won got to pick first. But my brother Steve won the boys' competition. There was a black labrador puppy named Slicer offered as a prize. Steve came up to me and said he wanted the dog, so I let him choose first. But we didn't know the puppy hadn't had his shots and we hadn't had him for very long when he died of distemper. Another lesson learned."

About that time Patty said to Ed Jones, "How 'bout my working for you on the range in exchange for practice balls to hit? He told me I wasn't old enough. Boy, was I crushed! In skiing I was never old enough to associate with the fifteen- and sixteen-year-olds. Now I wasn't old enough again, in spite of being older."

"Well," said Ed, "my shagger has big, heavy trays and I don't think you can pick them up."

Pouting, Patty told him she would try. Ed still kids Patty about always overestimating herself.

Did Ed Jones immediately recognize Patty Sheehan's athletic talents? "I can't honestly say that I said, 'Oh boy, here's a winner!'" It was difficult for Ed, working with small hands and large impatience.

But Bobo Sheehan had instilled a competitive will in his youngest athlete. Among his indelible quotes were:

"There's no sense competing if you're not going out to win.

"There's only one spot in athletics, and that's winning."

In her first ski race after the Sheehans had moved west, Patty beat all the boys. The boys included McLane McKinney, who was the older brother of Tamara McKinney, an Olympic skier. That year Patty Sheehan entered eleven races and won ten. In the race she lost, she caught a ski tip coming out of the starting gate. She spun around and started to cry. Bobo was there and yelled "Boot it!" Translated from ski vernacular, that means "Get going!" Patty dutifully took off and skied as hard as she could, finishing fourth. Leslie and Bobo had taught their daughter never to give up.

At the age of thirteen, however, the Olympic-skiing hopeful suddenly decided she'd had enough—the very same year she was named Most Outstanding Racer on the Far West Ski Association Ski Team. But skiing had become boring. Boot packing got old fast. "Consider, too, that by the time I was thirteen, I had already raced for nine years. Mother still thinks I gave up a good chance in skiing," Patty says.

Bobo differed. "I was the happiest guy in the world when Patty quit competitive skiing." Some newspaper reports have insisted that Bobo was disappointed with Patty's decision. He was not. "In a split second, you can be maimed for life." Remember Jill Kinmont? She was Patty's heroine. But Jill was a world-class ski champion one moment—and an instant later, a paraplegic.

Besides, Bobo observed, ski racers in the United States didn't earn the respect the Europeans stars did. "When Austrian Toni Sailer won three golds in the '56 Olympics in Cortina, he became a national hero." In this country if you were a ski racer, Bobo added, people thought it was because you couldn't get a job.

So Bobo was pleased Patty made the decision. No more hauling her around to ski meets, equipping her with four pairs of skis and all of the rest of the paraphernalia skiers require. No more hassle to mail meet entries in on time. No more worrying about Patty busting herself up. Nurturing Olympic dreams just wasn't worth the struggle. (By reason of both skill and luck, Patty never had a serious ski injury.)

"I will say this about my ski career," says Patty. "My parents never pushed me. As a coach, Dad had seen too many kids rebel when faced with parental pressure. They just encouraged me."

Bobo had said, "Patty, you can go as far as you want to go."As Patty grew through her ski-less teens, golf was becoming more a part of her life. She was even going to tournaments by herself.

Patty gives a firsthand account of one unchaperoned journey: "I was in the mall at a bookstore, before I had to be at Wooster High School to catch the bus to the Nevada State High School Golf Championship in Las Vegas. I was sniffing around the shelves trying to find something to read on the long trip when I spotted a golf book. The bus ride to Vegas went quickly. The golf book I selected was called *The Happy Hooker*. Boy, was I naive!"

By the time Patty Sheehan was sixteen, she had won three straight Nevada state high school championships. Before she was twenty, she had won four Nevada state women's championships, the last one by thirty-nine strokes.

When Patty was eighteen, she concluded it was time to get a job. Delivering the morning paper was the ideal chore because she could deliver papers at night and play golf during the day. At 2:00 A.M. she'd pick up the papers at the *Nevada State Journal* loading dock. Then she'd proceed to the parking lot to roll them up and wind the rubber band around them "really tight." Instructions on where to deliver them were on a cassette tape recorded by her supervisor.

"At one point I had to get out of my car, put the papers in bags, and deliver to each of the apartments in a big building." By 7:00 A.M. Patty was back in bed.

"When people would call because they didn't get their paper, brother Steve—next oldest from me—would deliver them for me. What a guy! Still is! Boy! Were those customers surprised to see a boy delivering their papers when all along they thought they had a paper*girl*."

Patty attended the University of Nevada at Reno three years, prodded by the simple motivation that she wanted to stay home. "I was not grown up enough to leave. I was not ready. Besides, the price was right at home: love, room, board— no charge. Also I was extremely shy. I didn't want to leave Mommy and Daddy."

Patty attributes her youthful shyness to her outgoing older brothers. "They were the leaders. I just tagged along with them, hanging back. They took care of me. A bus driver yelled at me for standing up in the bus the first day of school. I couldn't see out. I wanted to see out, the first

day of school. After that Steve walked me to kindergarten. He was seven."

During her third year at UNR, light bulbs snapped on and Patty realized she needed another school. UNR's women's golf program was nonexistent. When she went to tournaments, they'd get some coach from some other school to chaperone her, at no cost to UNR. "I had to have a chaperone," explained Patty, "not because I was naughty, but because it was the law."

Patty was scarcely treated like the state treasure she was.

Patty realized the futility of trying to negotiate with the athletic staff at University of Nevada for a better program. The Federally legislated Title IX, mandating equal opportunities in colleges and universities for women athletes, had been in effect for two years. Nevada officials administered as though they had never heard of it. Patty said, "I started looking around for another school. I just wasn't getting to play enough at University of Nevada."

She was offered a scholarship at the University of Tulsa, a women's golf powerhouse. Oozing with oil money and dripping with Lear jets, Tulsa sent the jets around the country to lure players from distant locales, such as Roswell, New Mexico, where a kid named Nancy Lopez lived. Pretty heady stuff, having a multimillion-dollar executive jet bring recruiters to you. Patty remembers, "I was looking hard at Tulsa. We played the intercollegiate there in Oklahoma in 1979. I was within one day of signing. The day after the tournament ended I was supposed to go to the campus and register for classes. But I decided Tulsa wasn't right for me. For one thing the golf team was away from school for weeks at a time. On one trip the players were away from campus for six weeks. I didn't figure I'd get much education there.

"But now I had to tell Dale McNamara, the Tulsa coach, that I had decided not to go there. That was something else, telling Dale. She kind of reminds me of pictures of Queen Victoria. She was a lady very properly in control of things. Taking a deep breath, I said, 'Dale, I've got something to tell you and you're not going to like it, but I've decided to go home and think this out.'"

So Patty returned to Reno, and the Sheehans scheduled a family conclave. Leslie said, opening the meeting, "San Jose is only about a five-hour drive from Reno."

Bobo added, "San Jose is close to skiing."

"And from playing amateur golf, I have a lot of friends in the San Jose area," Patty said.

So in 1979 Patty wrote Mark Gale, then coach at San Jose State, and told him she wanted to go there. She had enjoyed the company of their players, Juli Simpson, Carol Conidi, Shelley Flanagan, Kellie Swank, and Iris Andre. They had a great women's golf program with a good competitive schedule. SJSU had good players, too, who played different golf courses, good golf courses. It was the best move Patty Sheehan ever made. Patty was not without a scholarship for any period of time, even though she was what is called a "walk on"—someone who voluntarily shows up, who isn't recruited for a team.

Although a degree from San Jose State for his golfers was not a high priority item for Coach Gale, it was the San Jose State experience that really launched Patty Sheehan's big-time competitive golf career.

Dale McNamara, writing on University of Tulsa stationery, congratulated Patty on her choice of schools and wished her happiness and success. "Really a classy letter," Patty said.

The San Jose State team members, especially Carol Conidi, a bright, young business major, pulled all the stops to make Patty feel welcome. Carol showed her around the campus, took her to the airport when she needed to go home or go to tournaments. "And there *were* a couple of times that first semester that I really needed to go home!"

The first semester was not a carnival of fun for Patricia. "It took me a while to adjust to a new situation. It was hard to adjust to being on a *team*. I'd always been an individual. And there I was, having to wear the sa-a-ame uniform, looking the sa-a-ame, going to dinner with the sa-a-ame people, having a coach trying to tell you what to do. That was probably the worst part about it. I just can't take help or criticism from people whose golf knowledge I don't respect.

"Now, this isn't to say Mark Gale is not a nice guy. He is. But he didn't have all that much golf knowledge. He'd read an article in a golf magazine and then come out to practice and have *all* of us try it. When I was there he'd read an article about chipping by putting the toe of a number 6- or number 7-iron on the ground and chipping from that position. He didn't seem to understand that people can't all play the same way. Some coaches just don't consider you as an individual; they kind of give blanket instruction. My swing isn't going to work for everyone."

Patty won back-to-back California Amateur Championships in 1977 and 1978. She was runner-up in the National Amateur in 1979. She won the National Intercollegiate Championship in 1980. Also that year she won four matches while representing the United States in the international Curtis Cup matches. And she led the LPGA qualifying, shooting a 77–71–74–74 for a 296, six strokes ahead of Beverly Davis-Cooper at 302.

Patty did not graduate from San Jose State University, or from anywhere else (though she was later awarded an honorary doctorate by Middlebury College). Leslie Sheehan called Patty's then-manager, Margaret Leonard, and asked her to look into Patty's progress toward her degree. Margaret called the SJSU women's athletic director, Mary Zimmerman, who looked over Patty's transcripts. Mary reported that Patricia Leslie Sheehan had completed twenty units of golf and one academic course, and thus was a light year away from graduating. Mary was wrong, very wrong. Patty had transferred seventy-four units from the University of Nevada to San Jose State, had acquired only five units of golf (all A's, not surprisingly) and thirty-five units of required academic courses for a total of 109 units, only fifteen short of graduation.

"I have no clue as to how Mary thought I remained eligible," Patty said. "Under the rules of AIAW, the women's intercollegiate athletic association, an athlete had to make normal progress toward a degree. That means twelve units a semester."

Will Patty ever return to school to complete that one semester? For what possible reason?

Deciding to become a professional was a far more tortuous decision than going away to school was. Patty had asked Ed Jones in 1979 if the time had come for her to turn pro. He said bluntly, "You're not ready. You're not mature enough."

A few months later she asked her SJSU golf teammate, Juli Simpson, "Should I turn pro?"

Juli Simpson Inkster has always been a straight shooter. "What else are you going to do with your life?" was her answer.

What else, indeed. Patty, a degreeless major in human performance. ("Human performance" is just a fancied-up name for physical education.) The human performance she needed to demonstrate, she finally decided, was her own golf game subjected to the test of the LPGA tour.

"I won the National Intercollegiate Championship in late spring of 1980. I became a professional golfer the following day, June 14, 1980, my parents' wedding anniversary."

On that day the childhood of Patricia Leslie Sheehan ended.

WHEN THERE'S NOT TIME TO WARM UP

Betty Hicks wrote in her anecdotal cookbook, *Travels with a Golf Tour Gourmet,* a rather amusing depiction of a ladies day golfer on her way to the club. I understand her sister, Margaret Zimmerman, who plays at La Cumbre Country Club in Santa Barbara, didn't particularly appreciate the description. Here's an excerpt from Betty's book.

I learned very early in my golf career to exploit the competitive advantage advised by Walter Hagen: move very slowly before you play golf, from the moment you arise in the morning.

My sister, 22-handicapper Margaret Zimmerman, demonstrates the antithesis of Hagen's advice. She is joined in this rapid ritual by house

WHEN THERE'S NOT TIME TO WARM UP
continued

wife/golfers everywhere. She'll prepare a five-course make-ahead dinner for VIP company, pay the household bills, feed the horses, fertilize the camellias, drop the dog off at the vet's and still make her 8:14 tee time for the LaCumbre Country Club's member-guest tournament. Then she wonders why she has problems on the first few holes.

Obviously, Margaret had no time to hit a few practice balls.

There's a club at an Arizona retirement community where you'll see egg cartons scattered all over the practice range. *Egg* cartons? Sure, the shop will sell you one dozen practice balls in an egg carton, perfect for a quick warm-up. "Not too shabby an idea, really," says Ed Jones.

What if you don't even have time for an egg carton's worth? There are a couple of options. You really should stretch (see pages 43–45). Stretching will help you prevent injury and will improve your early shots because you'll be able to take a better turn.

Then there are various ways of making the club feel lighter when you tee off. Golf club manufacturers make training clubs, which are also good to help you strengthen golf muscles. Ben Hogan used to swing a weighted club (probably about twenty-two ounces) twenty minutes a day. Lacking a training club, you might see if your shop stocks those doughnut-shaped weights that slip right over the neck of your club. At one time a manufacturer made head covers that had lead weight in them. A golfer swinging a weighted club is the same as a ballplayer swinging three baseball bats. Swinging three clubs, however, is rather cumbersome. Try one of the types of weights instead.

STRETCHING EXERCISES

Neck Stretch
Either sit or stand.

1. Allow your chin to drop to your chest.	2. Slowly lift your chin and turn it over your left shoulder.	3. Return your chin toward the center of your body; then turn your right shoulder.

Trunk Stretch 1
Stand with feet about shoulder width apart

1. Let your arms hang at your sides with your palms facing your thighs.	2. Slide your left hand down the side of your left thigh. Go as far as you can toward your left knee. Repeat six times.	3. Repeat the procedure on your right side.

WHEN THERE'S NOT TIME TO WARM UP
continued

Shoulder Stretch I
Sit or stand.

1. With hands about shoulder width apart, grasp a golf club horizontally, palms facing downward.

2. Lift the club straight out in front of you. Keeping your arms extended, raise the club above your head.

3. Slowly bring the club down behind your head and neck as far as possible.

Shoulder Stretch II
Start in a standing position with your feet slightly apart.

1. Press each end of a short iron in the palm of each hand, allowing your arms to hang loosely in front of you.
2. Press with your left hand so the club and your right hand move directly out to your right and up. Your upper right arm will press gently against the right side of your head to allow you full motion.
3. Repeat the exercise on your left.

Trunk Stretch II
Stand with your feet shoulder width apart.

1. Hold a club behind you, parallel to the ground, in the crook of both elbows.
2. Slowly turn your shoulders and trunk to the left on the same plane as your shoulders turn in your swing.
3. Repeat the exercise to your right.

ON PRACTICING

"Everybody's different," says Ed.

"I sure agree," is my response. "We're not all Ben Hogans or Sandra Palmers, who beat on golf balls all day long. Maybe there's something in that Fort Worth, Texas, water!" (Ben and Sandra are both from Fort Worth.) "The big question is, 'How much practice?'"

"Depends somewhat on your B.D.—your burning desire—how much you're going to practice."

I don't practice much. That doesn't mean I don't have the B.D. In professional golf there are practicers (Tom Kite and Sandra Palmer), and there are players (Ben Crenshaw and myself). How often I've seen our tour players, after a bad round, go to the practice

ON PRACTICING
continued

tee and hit a couple of buckets of balls. I don't know what they are accomplishing. I like to work out a problem by just getting my feel back. Twenty to thirty minutes of swinging at balls usually does it for me.

Ed adds, "Just practice to a point where you don't get bored and disinterested. If you do, pack it up for the day and take a walk."

But why do golfers get bored and disinterested? Probably because they don't have a purpose when they practice. They just buy a bucket of balls, take them to the tee line, and bang them out with their woods. Beginners especially don't know diddly about practice.

Warm up with a half-pitching wedge shot. Work up to your woods. Then make your practice meaningful. Practice as though you're playing your favorite golf holes. This won't have to be completely in your imagination. If the driving range where you practice is any good as a facility, you'll have flagsticks to aim at, and maybe even target greens. And you'll have a nearby practice putting green.

Hit a drive. Then put your wood club back in your bag, and take out whatever iron you would hit for your second shot. Mix up the clubs, just as you would have to do on the golf course.

One of the major reasons golfers can't take their practice shots onto the golf course with them is that they don't practice realistically—like they're playing a round of golf. Practice! Don't just beat on golf balls.

"ALL I WANT IS . . ."

More distance and greater consistency. Ask a teaching professional what phrase he or she hears most often from women students on the lesson tee and it will probably be, "All I want is more distance and greater consistency." This is from women golfers with handicaps from ten to forty. Dream on! That's all I want! Another twenty yards on the drives and a lower scoring average brought about by improved consistency in shot-making. These are not, however, unachievable goals, especially for women golfers in the handicap range mentioned. But they do require a commitment of time and effort.

Here are some pretty typical comments I've heard from women golfers on the subject of achieving more distance:

"Size doesn't matter, does it?"

"It can't be strength; it must be timing."

"But it looks so easy. Those long hitters don't swing hard at the ball at all."

Size *does* matter. Do you think Laura Davies, at five foot, ten inches, doesn't have an advantage over me at five foot, three inches? Yes, size matters.

And strength matters. Without timing, of course, strength is wasted, but distance is dependent upon the speed with which you swing the clubhead, assuming good contact with the ball. Clubhead speed results not only from properly coordinated movements of the swing but also upon muscular strength.

Betty Hicks wrote in *Golf Digest* magazine forty years ago, "The average woman golfer with limited strength, with little prior sports experience which involves an aggressive attitude toward the object she wants to strike, and with precious little time to devote to practice, is confronted with a difficult problem when she seeks more distance."

Difficult, but not impossible. Here are hints, some of which happily will involve little or no effort on your part:

"ALL I WANT IS . . ."
continued

1. Make sure you are using the right type of golf ball for your swing. Consult your golf professional.

2. Are your clubs right for you—for your stature, for your strength, for your swing? Again, consult your teaching professional. Don't fall for the ladies' clubs/men's clubs limitation. This restriction can keep you from using clubs which fit you. Clubs that fit the player—custom-made clubs—once carried very high price tags. These days you can purchase clubs that fit at the usual retail price.

3. Learn and use the principles applicable to attaining distance. You should swing on every shot as fast as you can rhythmically swing. There are many distance-robbing cliches rampant in golf, many of them mouthed by well-meaning husbands and boyfriends. "Just hit the ball easy. Distance will come later." Much, much later. There is, of course, a point beyond which you cannot swing faster and still swing to waltz music. However, dismiss the idea that a good swing is effortless. Ever get a good view of the faces of good players when they're striking a drive? Those faces reveal effort! A good swing appears deceptively effortless because there are no extraneous motions (no "racing the motor") and because it is rhythmic.

4. Forget the word "relaxation" in reference to your golf swing. An expert kinesiologist (muscle specialist) friend of mine once said, "You cannot totally relax any major muscle group and still hit the golf ball. What you want is minimum tension."

5. Discuss with your teaching professional the advisability of the unlap or ten-fingered grip, sometimes called the baseball grip in error. (You would not grip a baseball bat that way, with your left thumb inside your right palm.) For women players who have small and/or weak hands, the

unlap offers some important advantages. Try not to buy the idea that the overlapping grip unites the hands and makes them work as one. They'll work as one as long as they're affixed to the same club shaft. The unlap grip, once you're used to it, will give you a mechanical advantage, the physics of which we'll leave to those golf machine folks to analyze.

6. Purchase and use a weighted training device or club. If you have an old, not-yet-antique wood club in your attic or garage, take it to a competent club repair shop (or you may have a club repairman living in your household) and direct the craftsman to increase the weight of the club to around twenty-one or twenty-two ounces. How does the repairman do that? He or she will remove the sole plate of the club, heat up a dish of lead, drill out some cavities in the club's sole, and pour in the melted lead. Lead tape is also available to press on the exterior of the club, usually on the club's back edge, but that will change the aerodynamics of the club. Maybe aerodynamics doesn't matter if you are not trying to hit the ball with the club.

7. Have a swing diagnosis to make sure you are "hitting on all fours"—that is, you are using every power-producing part of your body, especially your legs. Most of the women golfers I play with in LPGA pro-ams use their legs, but they use them just to *stand on*. Legs have a powerful role to play in the golf swing.

"How often," Ed Jones asks me, "have we worked from here—" Ed points to my right hip, "—to here?" He points to my right knee.

To use your legs effectively, your right knee must remain flexed on the backswing and your weight must—while the weight shifts to the right foot on the backswing—remain on the inside of the right foot. A teaching aid might help you here. Mickey Wright used a doorstop under the outside of her right instep. That was before more sophisticated devices had been invented, like Natural Swing Products' Stabilator. You will need to work with your teaching professional on correct use of legs in the swing.

CHAPTER THREE

IGNITING THE B.D.

The early 1980s were busy times for Patty Sheehan. They were among her most successful years in golf, if success is measured in prize money won and tournament victories. She was busy setting goals and meeting them. She was busy banking her prize money. Patty adds, "I was also busy putting my life back together after I'd lost my definition of it."

In Wheeling, West Virginia, at her first tournament after becoming a golf professional, Patricia won $400. Then she flew to Toronto and took in almost $1,000. From there it was west to Denver for the Columbia Savings Classic where, because she was shooting low numbers, she was paired with some of the tour's big names, such as Pat Bradley. Patty remembers, "Pat did not scare me at all. Pat Bradley is a nice person, one of my favorites to play with. I was pleased to find I was not intimidated by the stars of the tour. After all, I had played amateur and collegiate golf with Nancy Lopez, Debbie Massey, Chris John-son, Beth Daniel, and Juli Inkster, to name a few." Accustomed to the atmosphere of near-mile-high Reno, Patty enjoyed playing in mile-high Denver, Colorado. She shot five successive nines of 35, and only a missed 18-incher on the eighteenth the last day gave her a 36 and stopped her string. Tying for fourth, Sheehan won $5,100! "I was rich!" Patty exulted.

"Now I can live comfortably," Patty told *Denver Post* reporter Dorothy Mauk. "And get some good food." She implied the $5,100 would last to eternity and provided no clues about what she had been eating that made her crave gourmet fare.

In 1981 Patty won her first LPGA tournament, the Mazda Classic in Japan. She startled golf fans inter-nationally by turning a somersault on the eighteenth green following her title-winning long putt from off the green. It was a spontaneous, joyful act that may have horrified game purists.

Patty was named LPGA Rookie-of-the-Year in 1981, for winning the Mazda Classic, finishing eleventh on the money list, and winning $118,463 with a scoring average of 72.52.

"I wanted to do even better in 1982," she confesses. "I did. I won in Orlando. I won the SAFECO Classic in the Seattle suburb of Kent. I won the Inamori Classic back home in San Jose. My scoring average was 71.72, an improvement of 0.8 of a stroke." When a player's average is around par, cutting off strokes is far tougher than it is for a golfer shooting in the nineties or hundreds. Patty won $225,022 in 1982 and jumped to fourth place on the money list. But, no longer a rookie, she wasn't named anything-of-the-year.

Patty continued to nurture the B.D. What's the B.D.? This author has written about it:

Betsy Rawls and I were laboring on the practice tee of California's Riviera Country Club one off-season day in 1953. A distinguished-appearing gentleman sauntered up and watched a few swings. "It's obvious you both have it," he finally said. "I wouldn't give a darn for any of my players who didn't have it—the burning desire."

After he had walked up the hill to the first tee, I whispered to Betsy, "That was Frank Leahy!"

Betsy had also recognized one of Notre Dame's most revered football coaches. "Yeah, that's what does it; that's what it takes—the B.D."

We laughed and then chorused, "The B.D.," and referred to the Burning Desire thereafter, our own secret ingredient.

Since that day I've been vigilant for the B.D.—that marvelous intangible—in kids coming up. The B.D. is revealed by a certain glint in the eye, a give-away set of the jaw, a purposeful stride, a style of addressing the ball that makes an onlooker know, as Harvey Penick said, that "Hitting the golf ball is the most important thing in the world to that player right now."

For many players, great futures have been predicted by media people and golf professionals whose forecasts were made without punching Frank Leahy's secret ingredient into their forecasting computers.

A young woman may have a putting touch like spreading a hot Southern biscuit with honey, a tee shot that devours fairways,

iron shots which rattle flag-
sticks. And she may win, but
she won't go on winning, not
without the B.D.

There was a youngster from
Reno I met on professional Eddie
Jones' Hidden Valley Country
Club practice tee in '71. Later I
was to chaperone her to intercol-
legiate tournaments, because
Patty Sheehan was the only
player the University of Nevada
had, and the very few tourna-
ments they sent her to, they sent
her coachless, scarcely treating
her like the state treasure she
was, a new Nevada Mother
Lode.

"Gosh!" exclaimed one of my
San Jose State players, Carol
Conidi, "Patty really smokes
'em!" Carol had just completed
a practice round with the
Nevadan as they prepped for the
1977 National Intercollegiate
Championship at Hawaii's
Kuilima, on the northern tip of
Oahu.

But more important even
than her "smoked" tee shots,
her impeccable golf swing, her
magical putting, was Patty's
B.D. She exuded it. "This young
woman," I told myself, "is
going to be great." But I could-
n't tell anyone why Patty Shee-
han was going to be great.

Because no one but Betsy Rawls
and I would understand that
secret code of golf immortality
—the B.D.

Patty admits, "Once in a while I think about the B.D., especially when I'm in a tournament and feel the B.D. is flickering a little."

For Patty the early eighties were spectacular years. In 1982 she won $50,000 in the J and B Gold Putter Award, beating Pat Bradley 5 and 4 in the match play final. She achieved a major goal in 1983: she was named LPGA Player-of-the-Year after winning her first major—the LPGA Championship—along with three other tournaments. The year 1984 was no letdown; Patty won the Vare Trophy for lowest scoring average (71.40) along with four tournaments. That same year she won the biggest bonus in golf histo-ry, $500,000 for consecutive wins in the McDonald's Kids' Classic and the LPGA Championship. In 1985 Patty passed the $1 million mark in winnings, the first of her million dollar marks.

While she was enjoying these successes, Patty also confronted a very major personal crisis. "I had lost the definition of what my life is supposed to be about. I had to get away—just *had to*—get away from the tour. Golf had ceased being fun for me," Patty explains succinctly.

"I was unhappy and frustrated," she told a *Washington Post* writer, Doug Cress. "Everything I'd worked so hard for wasn't fun anymore. I felt a lot of pressure to be the best player in the world and to be the best representative possible for the LPGA. Everyone wanted a piece of me. I couldn't just be myself anymore. I guess it was a classic case of burnout."

Being disqualified in the 1981 LPGA Championship for an illegal drop from a water hazard on the final round's sixteenth hole could have been a precipitating factor in Patty's leaving the tour. It's an embarrassment being charged with an illegal drop when you believe the drop you are making conforms to *The Rules of Golf*. A golf professional is supposed to know the rules, right? Even with a one-penalty stroke for the drop, Patty shot a last round of 66. Her prize money would have been $4,600.

Patty told her manager, Margaret Leonard, an attorney in Santa Cruz, California, and longtime friend from college golf, "I'm the best in the world. There is nowhere for me to go but down."

Margaret Leonard told Doug Cress, "Patty's entire approach to the game and everything associated with it had become negative."

So Patty said good-bye to the LPGA tour with a faint "tah, tah" and went home to Los Gatos and her beloved condominium for five weeks. She became a recluse—an introspective recluse.

She figured out that the values that guided her mother and father in raising her mattered more than all the tournament wins, the Rolex watches, or the prize money. "My LPGA ranking didn't mean diddly unless I had my self-worth. My self-worth had eroded on the tour."

She allowed herself a pair of golf diversions during those weeks. She galleried the U.S. Men's Open at Pebble Beach and, toward the end of the five weeks, she hit a few golf balls.

The timeout was fruitful. "When I went back on the tour five weeks later, I felt really relaxed. I started playing aggressively again, rippin' it for the flagsticks, knockin' the back of the cup out on putts. That's my style. It's what I expect of myself." Patty hates losing. She enjoys seeing her name on the leader board. "When I'm playing I'm having a good time. When I'm playing well, I'm having a better time."

In the *Post*, Cress observed, "It's hard to appreciate the strength it took for Sheehan to admit she had become engulfed by golf, unless you understand the fury with which she attacks the game, and for that matter, life itself." The word "fury" in this instance had nothing to do with anger, and everything to do with intensity.

Patty's closest friends say that she is driven to succeed. True. The B.D. creates impossible standards, standards that are unreachable. Clare Sheils, who was Patty's press agent from 1982 to 1989 and public relations coordinator for the LPGA for two years before that, told her, "You really can't conceive there is anything you can't do in golf, can you?"

"Nope, nothing." Patty Sheehan did want to be the best; she wanted it badly. She wanted it so badly she could taste it—bittersweet, vinaigrette, sweet and sour, that was how it tasted.

It was inevitable that during Patty's early years on the tour she was introduced to what is loosely known as social life on the tour. Tour social life is distinct from homebound social life. The tour life is going to cocktail parties and out to dinner with people you barely know. It's superficial. It's small talk. It's groupies drooling over autographs. True, the LPGA's fans are necessary to the tour's prosperity, but that doesn't mean they translate into a social life.

Tour social life lacks the down home warmth of people's social life whose work lets them remain in one spot geographically, lets them interact honestly with friends around the same fireplace on every Saturday night, lets them turn the same key in the same lock each day to find refuge from the workaday world.

The hotel people who developed the residence inn concept—hotel suites with kitchens and other amenities that make them seem more like home—are heroes to LPGA tourists. These hotels allow pets, too, which allowed Sherlock and Quincey, Patty's two very small poodles weighing in at eight pounds each (one white, one black), to go on tour.

There isn't really time and energy for social life on the tour, yet the fans expect that you will *have* a social life. Everybody has a social life, right? Sandra Palmer said it best. "When you hit golf balls all day you don't much feel like jumpin' around all night."

There's an eerie kind of uncertainty that accompanies waking up in the morning and having to ask yourself, "What town am I in today?"

"Oh, yeah, I'm in Duluth, Georgia, where nightmares are born."

Or, "I'm in Corning or Rochester, New York, where dreams come true."

It did not take many years for the tour life to start grinding on Patty. She told Mike Penner of the *Los Angeles Times* that the tour was getting to be a job. "It gets old after a while," she said. "You're always eating out. That really bothers me. Everything starts to taste the same. Everything you eat is loaded with salt and fat. It's tough to have a good diet when you're on the tour.

"Plus, you're not sleeping in your own bed. You're wearing the same clothes all the time. That gets to be boring." At least, when she started wearing knickers at the urging of Head Sportswear, getting dressed in the morning became a trifle more interesting.

In these early years on the tour Patty developed a reputation for her aversion to practice. She may go all winter, during the tour's tournament lull, without hitting a golf ball. "I'll go skiing. I'll putter around the house. I'll take the dogs for runs. I'll cook a gourmet dinner. If the mood hits, I'll drive out to Hidden Valley, hit a bucket of practice balls, have Ed Jones look at my swing."

The other players tease her about her lack of a work ethic. There's a doltish tradition in golf that unless a player practices until her hands bleed, as Babe Zaharias allegedly did (although there are no witness-

es), she isn't really practicing. If Patty has a round in which she's hit the ball badly (by her demanding standards), she may go to the practice tee for fifteen or twenty minutes after the round to reestablish her feel. She works it out in that length of time.

If other players see her starting on her second bucket of practice balls, they'll say, "Oh, you're getting serious about this game."

"I think you can practice so much you lose your objective. I think some players go to the practice tee just to be seen there, to let the others know they're working at the game," Patty observes.

In the early 1980s the media started giving her "superstar" status. She did not feel comfortable with that appellation. She joked with reporters by saying, "Sure and begorrah, I'm the greatest Irish player ever to come out of Reno, Nevada."

But insistent reporters pointed to her brief amateur career. She'd won four Nevada State Amateurs and two California State Amateurs. She was Collegiate All-American for three years, won the National Intercollegiate in 1980, was runner-up in the National Amateur, and won all four of her matches in the international Curtis Cup competition. She was the leading point-winner on the United States team. Then, after leading the qualifying by six strokes, she hit the LPGA tour, a white tornado ripping up records, scooping up prize money and honors, rudely shoving aside Nancy Lopez, Amy Alcott, Pat Bradley, Sandra Haynie, Kathy Whitworth, and other established stars.

"I never think of myself as a superstar," she told Gene Caddes of UPI after her win in the LPGA Championship in 1983. "I'm just out here playing golf. Being a superstar is not one of my goals."

Rejecting the superstar label, Patty analyzed her capabilities. "The best thing I have going for me, I believe, is my attitude." Patty Sheehan's attitude is a syndrome, not a single attribute. She is confident. She has a good time on the course. She doesn't take the Royal and Ancient Pastime too seriously. "If I had to name any one part of my game that gives me a big advantage over other players, it's my concentration." Ed Jones says he has seen two golfers who concentrate better than anyone else he's observed. One is Ben Hogan. The other is Patty Sheehan.

"Patty Sheehan is going to be so good, it's scary," JoAnne Carner said in 1984.

"I still don't want to be a superstar," Patty commented. Superstars are put on unrealistic pedestals. Patty did not belong on a pedestal. "I did not want to be there, out of everyone's reach."

A headline in *Golf World* magazine in 1983 read, "Only Patty Sheehan Thinks She's No Superstar." Patty Sheehan was outvoted.

Nine years later, the great Kathy Whitworth, who should really understand the definition of "superstar," having won eighty-eight times on the LPGA tour, said at Patty Sheehan's induction into the LPGA Hall of Fame, "Patty fought being a superstar. I'm glad to see her become—for Patty's sake—the great player I knew she could be."

The greatness was probably best articulated in Patty's birdie blitzes. She would shoot three in a row, four in a row, five in a row. She shot nine birdies in one round at the Corning Classic in 1983 en route to a 63 and a tournament record total of 16 under par. The gallery saw the putts she sank for those nine birdies—ten, three, three, twenty-five, twelve, two, twenty, three, four and twelve feet, in order. But what set up those birdie-length putts? Smoked drives down the middle, long irons to the heart of the greens, short irons to makeable distances, "stony" (up really close to the cup) wedges.

Mike Blackwell may not have been totally objective when he was writing about Patricia. After all, he was writing for the *Reno Gazette-Journal*, the hometown paper Patty peddled when she was eighteen. "Sheehan is a great athlete," he wrote in June of 1984. "Sheehan is a great golfer. Sheehan is a great person. Great this, great that, great everything. Such accolades sometimes gnaw on the young woman."

"Does being a great athlete make you a great person?" Blackwell asked Patty.

Patty answered, "I didn't think so, looking back on the antics of some great athletes I've known. It isn't automatic."

What "grawed" on Patty, as Mike called it, was the rip-off of her privacy. Patty treasured her privacy. She told Mike, "I don't like people knowing all about me and getting inside my life. Other than that, being in the limelight is nice."

Brother Butch defends his baby sister, perhaps too ferociously at times for Patty's taste, though she likes being defended by her oldest brother. "She has a very private life," Butch told Blackwell.

It was difficult for Patty, deciding to write this book. She said, "I think private lives are private. I don't like the current trend to tell-all type books. I especially don't like it when authors try to make big bucks scraping up dirt on famous people. And I think it's really lousy when they try to dig up dirt on dead people. If I want dirt, I'll go dig in my vegetable garden."

Patty has lived an exemplary life. Other than her temper tantrums over golf when she was a child, and the mischief she'd got into with her three brothers, there's nothing she needs to hide. "Oh, I cheated on a test once in high school," Patty has confessed. "I am really ashamed of that. I looked at someone else's paper, and to this day I don't know what compulsion made me do it. There the paper was, like a flag waving in front of me. And my eyes just were drawn to it, as though that paper was a magnet. I had not done that before, and I never did that again."

Any ordinary mortal would believe that probably a player would need a best friend on the tour, someone with whom to share the unknowns and the scariness and the pleasures.

It's very difficult to have a best friend on tour because the players are in a highly competitive business. It's natural they should get competitive with one another, but this competitiveness can take some very vicious turns. Bad-mouthing is probably the least hurtful of those turns. Trying to tear the other person down, when you're both playing a game which, by its nature, can destroy fragile self-esteem, is the worst of the repercussions. Patty learned about that destructiveness firsthand.

"I can't think of any examples of two top-ranked players who have remained best of friends for very long, traveling together, playing practice rounds together, critiquing one another's golf games, taking lessons from the same professional, dining together, maybe even sleeping together."

Or so the rumors go. Patty has her opinion. "And so what if they do, as long as they aren't hurting anyone? They certainly aren't guilty of overpopulating the world, or adding to the hordes of abused children, like those girls who live at Tigh Sheehan, the home I underwrote in Santa Cruz, California. There are just a lot of men who for some sick reason get titillated at the idea of two women making love. C'mon, guys! Grow up!"

The obsession of adult men with women's various body parts is something else about the male sex Patty fails to understand. "To me, it's kind of a bovine preoccupation. Excuse the pun, but I find it udderly ridiculous."

In Patty's first few years on tour, she was her own best friend. "I have to be," she told Bob Fowler of *USA Today*. "I've learned how to be content with myself. I don't have any boyfriends—actually, my social life stinks. I've just put any sort of relationship on hold until I quit the tour. I couldn't bear the thought of having someone special at home while I was out on the tour."

After Patty told Fowler, "I don't think of myself as feminine anyway," Bob appraised her in his own way: "Sheehan is petite and wholesome with sparkling blue eyes, and, although she may lack the glitter of Stephenson, she has natural charm." Thanks, Bob. Good to know cleavages are not required to be an attractive human being.

Fowler's compliments aside, Patty opted to go the tour alone. "That's the Vermonter in me, I guess. I became a loner on the tour in the early '80s." The *USA Today* reporter observed most of Patty's competitors were in awe of her, but privately Patty knew she couldn't appeal to the public by unveiling her breasts on magazine covers like Jan Stephenson did. Patty smiles a lot on the golf course, and although Patty's is a nice smile, she doesn't have a smile that produces meltdowns in fans, like Nancy Lopez does. Patty has never practiced in front of a mirror, smiling and waving to the gallery as touring pro Debbie Meisterlin did. She doesn't crack one-liners like Big Mama Carner. Patricia is just the kid from next door.

As Bobo joked, "Patty's got her mother's butt and my boobs." Patty admitted, "I don't have a cleavage worth showing off."

"That's survival talk," Doug Cress from the *Post* wrote, "coming from a woman whose dedication to her craft has distorted her self-perception."

Patty responded, "Well, I don't know about that. I think those weeks I took away from the tour got my self-perception back in focus. I'd never really lost it. It just got kind of fuzzy."

An example of Patty's renewed peace of mind was the 1983 LPGA Player-of-the-Year banquet in New York. "It had been difficult to convince Sheehan to wear an evening gown and heels to the dinner," wrote reporter Cress, "although once there she accepted the award and accolades with modesty and grace."

Clare Sheils said of the evening, "We were so proud of her. We all knew how hard this sort of thing was for her." Clare also remembered that at one time in the evening, Patty, like ordinary mortals, had to go to the ladies room. Just then, the band broke into an up-tempo tune she couldn't resist.

It was like the somersault Patty did in Japan after she won her first tournament. That somersault just happened. And it just happened, there in New York at this very formal banquet, that Patricia just started dancing a funky little dance step all the way to the ladies room. "The rhythm got to me. The elation of the evening got to me."

A number of her fans have pointed out one obvious fact. In spite of all the honors she has collected, Patty has never been number one on the money list. It's not sour grapes that make her say that doesn't matter to her. She has been second five times, and that doesn't matter to her either. "I understand that money is awfully important to some people, and I like winning it, too. Billie Jean King used to say that others only looked at how much you made. In the case of golf, fans don't look at your scoring average, or top ten finishes, or how many tournaments you win, how many major titles you nail. Nope, they only care about the bucks you earned."

Money winnings are skewed statistics. The person who has good finishes in the tournaments that offer the big prize money, like the Sprint,

PATTY SHEEHAN'S AWARDS

1981	LPGA Rookie-of-the-Year
1983	Rolex LPGA Player-of-the-Year (determined by a point system)
1984	Vare Trophy for low scoring average (71.40)
1984	Seagram's Sports Award Woman Golfer of the Year
1985	Founder's Cup, given to the LPGA member who has made altruistic contributions to the betterment of society
1986	Samaritan Award, given to the LPGA player who during the last four years has most clearly demonstrated the selfless qualities of a good samaritan. The award acknowledges humanitarian, charitable efforts to improve human health or alleviate physical suffering
1987	*Sports Illustrated*'s Sportsmen of the Year (honored for humanitarianism along with seven other athletes)
1988	Charlie Bartlett Award, presented by the Golf Writers Association of America to a playing professional for unselfish contributions to the betterment of society
1989	All Set Hair Spray/Ladies Professional Golf Association Performance of the Year Award.
1994	Women's Sports Foundation Flo Hyman Award, for humanitarian contributions.

the McDonald's LPGA Championship, and the du Maurier, improve their chances of finishing high on the money list. Patty savors other honors—the Vare Trophy for lowest scoring average and the Rolex Player-of-the-Year Award. And Patty continues to treasure the Rolex Rookie-of-the-Year Award, though it has limited access, of course; a player is only a rookie for one year.

There are other awards, named for various people, Charlie Bartlett, Ben Hogan, Herb and Joe Graffis, Patty Berg, Bob Jones, William Richardson, Mary Bea Porter, and Heather Farr. Patty has earned many of them. She likes best the fact that several are for her humanitarianism, for making the world a better place. The awards and their criteria are given above.

"Sure, I'm pleased," Patty says, "not because I was praised in a very public way, but because of what I did to be nominated for the awards in the first place."

In 1984 Patty continued swinging well and won the LPGA Championship again, which made her and Mickey Wright the only back-to-back winners of this tournament. Furthermore, Patty beat Mickey's thirty-year-old record, winning by 10 strokes with a 16-under total of 272. She broke nine tournament records in two days when she finished 63–68. "I even impressed a few of my rivals. I'd rather impress Mickey Wright. She has always been an idol of mine. She is the ultimate woman golf professional: intelligent, personable, sensitive, and owner of the best golf swing the game has ever seen."

Patty's sister competitors were determined not to let her get big headed over her achievements. Beth Daniel was quoted as saying, "Patty knows how to win. She has that killer instinct. She proved that today. Before she can claim to be the best player in the world, though, she has some more to prove. She can be considered as one of the best players on tour now, but you have to look at a whole career to say you're the best. She hasn't been out here that long." Beth finished as runner-up in the LPGA Championship.

The media did little to spread the word about Patty's achievements. Jim Achenbach, writing in a Sarasota, Florida, newspaper called her "one of the best kept secrets in all of sports." He called her a "silent superstar" after she won the Sarasota Classic by edging out Nancy Lopez. "The Great Ice Lady," Achenbach called her as well, adding, "I am happy to report that the public perception of Sheehan is inaccurate. Although Sheehan has captured a total of thirteen titles in her five-year career and won the LPGA Championship back-to-back in 1983 and 1984, she remains a mystery woman. She appears cool and somewhat aloof. She displays stern concentration and an emotionless face on the golf course. Off the golf course, Sheehan is personable and talkative. She is engaging and intelligent. She is a winner."

Patty says in her own defense, "Hey, when I'm on the golf course I'm working. I'm at the office."

"In women's golf," Jim Achenbach wrote, "Sheehan sits on the summit."

COURSE MANAGEMENT

When Carl Laib, my tour caddie, pulled on his professor's cap and gown and lectured at Stanford University to the school's women's golf team during fall quarter, 1995, the subject was Course Management 101. Keeping an accurate yardage book was an important section of Carl's lecture.

Course management? It means you are in control of the golf course, rather than vice versa. It's like you're in a chess game. You're maneuvering for position. You need to know the pin placement before you tee off on a hole. You need to know the definition of phrases like "opening up the green." You need to know the differences between playing aggressively (sometimes rhymes with "stupidly") and playing conservatively. You must objectively evaluate the strengths and weaknesses of your game. And you must *think* on the golf course.

I believe I was introduced to course management when I started playing amateur golf tournaments. I watched a lot. I used to hit my driver off every tee, then I saw some of the players hitting 3-woods off the tee. "Ah, hah," I thought. "So *that's* course management!"

I'd just kind of copycat everybody. Nobody ever taught me how to do yardage. I'm not a great communicator. I always watched my brothers.

Can just any golfer apply the art and science of course management to his or her game? Any golfer can, although the greater the skill level of the player the more techniques can be applied. If you cannot predict within fifty yards where your shots may come down, applying course management becomes simply academic. Let's start with course management techniques that anyone of any handicap can apply:

1. Tee off on the side of the teeing ground closer to the trouble you are trying to avoid.
2. Rather than slowing down play by searching for those hard-to-find yardage markers on sprinkler heads, make

COURSE MANAGEMENT
continued

yourself a yardage book for your home course, or for courses you frequently play. The yardage book will relate objects
(usually trees) off the fairway to the sprinkler head distances. Example: at right angles across the fairway from a
sprinkler head that tells you it is 122 yards to the center of
the green is a slender cypress tree. The diagram of this hole
in your yardage book should inform you of that fact. See
page 67 for an example of a page from my yardage book
which Carl has developed for me.

3. Know that there's no rule in golf that states "thou shall
   shoot for the flagstick." Now, I like to go for it, but I am
   possibly more accurate with my irons than you are. Even
   so, going for it—the flagstick—has gotten me into trouble
   at times. I've lost tournaments because of not playing more
   conservatively. Particularly for high-handicap players, you
   need to tell yourselves that you have a better chance of getting down in three from your present position by *not going
   for the pin*. For example, there's a bunker between the flagstick and your ball. The cup is cut about twenty feet back
   from the edge of the green. A pitch to the right front of the
   green, followed by a chip from that position, and you're
   down in three. The possibility of really big numbers—double and triple bogeys—exists if you try to pitch over the
   bunker and stop the ball in those twenty feet of green.
   Unless you're a low-handicapper, you can't throw the big
   numbers off your score card; they have to be added!

4. Nor do you have to go for the pin out of bunkers, either!
   The higher face of a bunker will usually be between your
   position in the bunker and the flag. Yet most high-handi-
   cappers will go for the flag, catch the steep face of the
   bunker, and fail to get out until several efforts later. Did
   you ever consider going out sideways, in the direction

where the bunker is more shallow? Even hitting backwards can have appeal.

5. Learn how to read greens. Now, you don't have to read them as though you were reading *War and Peace*. Since ladies' groups at clubs these days emphasize playing faster, you will draw some angry stares if you try to line up your putts as though you were a touring professional. One time Betty Hicks was playing an exhibition with Bob Hope, whose caddie said to him, "Watch this green, Mr. Hope. It was mowed this morning." Quipped Bob, "What time?"

That's overkill. Hope humor, but overkill.

If you are not the first to putt in your group, you can be lining up your putt either from behind or from the side as your playing companions putt. Your ability to read greens has to be matched by your putting ability. There's little to be gained in knowing a sixty-foot putt will break $2^1/2$ inches to the left if you cannot stroke the ball within five feet of that spot. See my suggestions on reading greens on page 157.

You will play faster if you take two putts rather than four. Even an approximate read of the green will help you toward your two-putts goal.

COURSE MANAGEMENT FOR LOW- HANDICAP PLAYERS

Know where the pin is on every hole before you tee off so you can plan your tee shot to a position which opens up the green (gives you a clear shot to the pin, not impeded by bunkers or other hazards).

No, you do not have to hit a driver off the tee on every hole. If a fairway is narrow or if hazards are in the landing area, for your drive you may want to be more conservative. The exact distances to those hazards must be in your yardage book.

When Carl was working with the Stanford team they all had their drivers out preparing for a tee shot on the twelfth at Stanford Golf Club. The twelfth hole is a par 5 with a huge oak in the middle

COURSE MANAGEMENT
continued

of the fairway. There are bunkers on both sides of the fairway. "What would Patty hit here?" asked one team member. "Not driver!" Carl snapped. Four drivers went back into four golf bags. "Why bring those bunkers into play?" Carl Laib asked. "You can hit two 3-irons here on your first two shots, and then hit a full number 8-iron into the green."

"This is basic," lectured Professor Laib. "Play the hole the way it was designed. You don't want to leave yourself unmakeables."

"Why would you want to hit a full number 8-iron when you could be hitting a half wedge instead?" asked a Stanfordite.

"That full number 8 is more controllable. It's going to stop faster, all conditions equal, than is a half wedge.

"Did you ever consider why some tour players will hit it bad and shoot 74, and some will hit it bad and shoot 80?" Carl then asked the team. The answer was obvious: course management skills.

Remember that if you are trying to play short on a shot, you are likely to hit it longer than you ordinarily do, so you may want to take less club. How come? You'll swing smoother, knowing you aren't trying to hit it far. "Lay up" distances—the distance between your average shots and the hazard you want to avoid—are very important inclusions in your yardage book.

YARDAGE BOOKS

Carl becomes most eloquent on the subject of yardage books. Notice those little spiral-bound notebooks peeking out of tournament play-

Opposite: Typical pages from my yardage book. This one is from Bethesda Country Club and the Mazda LPGA Championship, which I won. If there is no significant difference in distance between the clubs in your set, a yardage book may not help you much. But when the professionals and low handicap players know exactly how far they hit with each club in their bags, yardage books help lower scores. Note the very precise yardages. Note, too, how Carl Laib made minute changes of as little as two yards to the basic yardages provided. J.I.C.Y.R.F.U. translates "Just in case you really (bleep) up." The upper part contains Carl's notes on what I hit each day and how far I hit it.

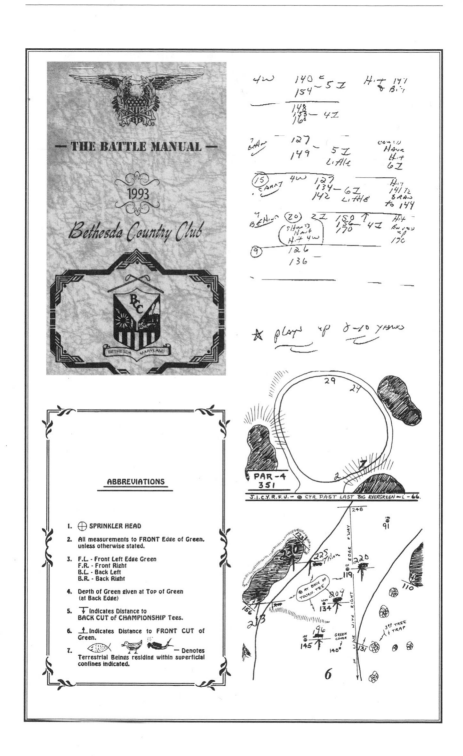

COURSE MANAGEMENT
continued

ers' back pockets? Those are yardage books. They are largely responsible for the low scoring on the professional tours today.

Carl advised, "The most important round you'll play during a tournament week is your practice round. You must walk the layout [course]. You must walk the greens. Your yardages must be *perfect.*"

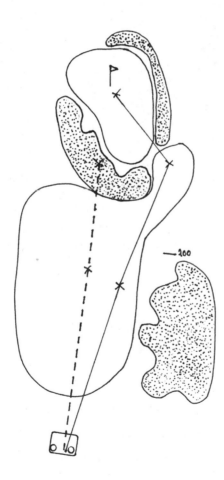

Diagram of a hole on which "big numbers" are a possibility for higher handicap players. There's no rule in golf that says you "gotta hit for the flagstick." You might be better off going the long way around, as shown here. Instead of following the dashed line as an impetuous player might, determined to hit the flagstick, the wise player manages the hole by opening up the green for herself, leaving an unobstructed third shot. The player who goes for the pin might well take two or more shots to get out of the bunker. The mid or high handicap player must know there is no rule mandating hitting for the flag.

"How come," asked a Stanford team member, "two players can pace off the same distance and come up with different yardages?"

"Because they haven't measured and taken their strides accurately. Your normal step isn't exactly three feet—or at least we hope it isn't, or you'd look pretty funny when you walk. When you're walking off yardage, other golfers will know that's what you are doing and won't laugh at your stride."

Carl's advice was to measure off a step of exactly thirty-six inches. Then remember how making that step *feels*. Practice making that stride. Then measure again. Even an error of a few inches will throw your yardage measurements off. Carl reemphasized: "Your yardages must be perfect."

Sprinkler head covers provide laser-measured yardages to the *center* of the green. Take half the length of the green (which you have previously paced for yardage) off that to find distance to the front. This is particularly useful information if the greens are hard and you need to bounce a shot in from the front edge.

Many higher-handicap women golfers hit close to the same distance with every club in their bags, and particularly with their irons. For them to benefit from knowing yardages, they must know the exact yardage they can hit their short irons (9 through 7), their middle irons (6 through 4), and their high-lofted fairway woods (9- through 5-woods). The yardage will probably be the same for each *grouping* of clubs. There may not be any difference between say, the 9-iron and the 8-iron, or between the 5-iron and the 6-iron. Why? Because these less skilled players simply do not swing with enough speed to exploit the difference in shaft lengths between each club in the set.

The solution? For starters, a weight training program might help. And no, it is highly unlikely the result will be bulging muscles. Your estrogen will protect you, ladies.

CARL LAIB ON PRACTICE

"There they were," said Carl Laib, "the Stanford women's golf team, out on the range, pounding balls and pounding balls. They should have been out on the course, chipping and putting."

COURSE MANAGEMENT
continued

If course conditions permit (no players are waiting behind you), chip from every angle into a green. "You need to know you can get it up and down when you miss a green," advised Carl. "Work on your chipping and putting." Unfortunately, practice chipping greens at most courses are flat and are not maintained to course standards, and thus do not provide realistic practice opportunities. Unfortunately also, most courses are so crowded in these days of peak golf popularity that on-the-course practice is difficult. Try early morning or late evening on-course practice.

HOW TO HIT 'EM HIGH

If you play golf long enough, you'll inevitably put your golf ball in a place from which you must hit a shot with a higher than normal trajectory to clear an obstacle, usually a tree.

"How do I hit it high, like over that aspen tree over there?" I asked Ed when I was about fourteen. "I don't think I could make it, even with the most lofted club I have in my bag."

Ed put out his left hand, fingers spread, and with the forefinger of his right hand, started counting the modifications.

"First, play the ball forward.

"Second, put your weight more on your right foot.

"Third, open up the clubface.

"And then, be sure you visualize the flight of the ball over that tree."

I continued to question Ed. "The shot distance calls for a number 7-iron," I observed. "Shouldn't I hit a number 6-iron, since I'm opening the face?"

"Right!" said Ed. "Now, let me see a high shot!"

Man! Did that shot soar! It looked like Mickey Wright had hit it. The ball went into orbit. Thanks, Ed.

PATTY AND BOBO TALK ABOUT *FEEL*

Dad and I often talk about sports techniques. Retired athletic coaches never really retire.

"*Feel* is hard to explain, isn't it?" I asked Bobo Sheehan. "But I think I know where it comes from. I think *feel* results from your upbringing."

"Well, we sure brought you up to be in tune with your body when you were a child," Dad explained. "And that's what it's all about—being in tune with your body."

"I know when I'm out of balance, for instance," I said. "But I sure have a hard time feeling where I am when I line up."

"Maybe Carl, your caddie, could line you up," Dad joked, knowing my dislike for having a caddie line up a tournament player.

I answered, maybe a bit angrily, "No thanks; if I can't do it myself it's not going to get done." Then I added, "But I sure have a good feel for distance. Maybe it's those great eyesight genes I inherited from you and Mom. My eyesight has deteriorated, though—to 20–20. I used to be 20–15 before all my gray hair came along. I sure can see terrain subtleties. Spose that comes from having to see that fall line in skiing?"

Dad agreed. "I sure think it might. You had to evaluate all those uphills and downhills and sidehills when you were skiing. Even though there's no snow on the ground, it's no different on the golf course. It all comes from knowing where that fall line is—which way gravity will take you on either side of that line."

Inevitably, someone will ask with what part of me I feel the golf swing. I feel with my body. I feel with my hands. I feel with my fingers. I can even feel in the swing, while I'm doing it, whether I am in a good or bad position.

I told Dad, "I can often make corrections in my swing during the swing itself. That ability comes from playing all those different sports when I was growing up. I know how to manipulate implements. When I hit a ball I can feel where my shots are going to go without even looking at the ball flight."

PATTY AND BOBO TALK ABOUT *FEEL*
continued

"'Feel' comes from your eyes, from the balance your body senses, from your tactile—your touch—senses," said the ol' Middlebury College and Olympic coach. "It all adds up to the *kinesthetic sense.* I think Mr. Webster defines it as *'A sense mediated by the end organs located in muscles, tendons, and joints and stimulated by bodily movements and tensions.'*"

"Yeah," I admitted, "I quit college when I just had one semester left to go, before I got to my kinesiology course, but I know kinesiology sure relates to my golf swing. You think *feel* can be taught, Dad?" I asked.

"Probably not," said Bobo Sheehan. "But to a certain degree, maybe your basic feel can be enhanced. If a person misses out on the early learning opportunities—and a lot of women do, by being deprived of sports experience as children—a golf teacher can give you exercises and drills to increase feel, like Ed Jones gave you when you were a kid."

(Exercises and drills are detailed in Chapter 1 and throughout the instructional series in *Patty Sheehan on Golf.*)

I remembered, "Ed Jones took my raw, undirected sense of feel and turned it into specific feel for the golf swing. Ed Jones, kinesiologist."

Edgar Milton Jones would just grin and say, "OK. How do you spell it?"

CHAPTER FOUR

RAIN DELAYS AND
RAINBOWS

Patty Sheehan has played in all twenty of the United States Golf Association Women's Opens since 1976 when she first entered as an amateur at Philadelphia's Rolling Green Country Club. It was not a happy week, perhaps an omen of Opens to come.

"Rolling Green's course was so-o-o-o long," Patty remembered of the 1976 Open. "I was all by myself and didn't know many people. The national bicentennial was being celebrated in the city, but I didn't have a car so I watched the festivities on the hotel TV." There were rain delays, another possible omen. Patty did not make the cut in Philadelphia; at least that outcome was not ominous. Patty has been runner-up three times and winner twice.

In 1977 the Open was contested at the Hazeltine Country Club outside of Minneapolis. "I was feeling so inadequate!" Patty recalled. "The pros paid no attention to you if they knew you'd probably not

make the cut. Furthermore, I didn't like to hang out in the locker room. Some players accused me of being antisocial. But the fact is that the locker room is not a very good hangout place. First, you tend to eat too much of their fattening buffets and then there's too much negative talk going on."

Negative talk examples:

"'How'd you like that pin placement on twelve? A six-foot break from either side.' I knew the break wasn't six feet. More like six inches.

"'Man! Is that OB close on number five!' There was actually plenty of room.

"'Didja ever get in that bunker in front of seventeen green? The Grand Canyon's just a puny divot in comparison.' That bunker was a carbon copy of our *shallow* practice bunker at Hidden Valley Country Club, back in Reno." Locker room talk blows the problems out of proportion. Patty says, "It gets you to thinking negatively, too. I try to shelter myself from that. I still feel the same way about the locker room, twenty years later."

The United States Golf Association's Women's Open is the most difficult tournament of the year. Patricia admits, "It's the one I've most wanted to win. I've spent much of my life preparing to win it, but so many different happenings have gotten in the way. The Open has produced many different emotions for me, like in '83, a positive experience even though I was second to Jan Stephenson. I played well.

"And I was proud of the way I played finishing as runner-up to Lisolotte Neumann in 1988. I shot 70–72–68–70 for a 280 total and lost to Lotte by 3 strokes. So my memories of the Open are vivid from the early years and vivid in the later years, but everything in between is sort of a fog."

The 1990 disaster is not foggy. The USGA's 1990 Women's National Open was played at the Atlanta Athletic Club's Riverside Course on the banks of the Chattahoochee River in the Atlanta suburb of Duluth.

Sports Illustrated entitled its one-page report on the tournament "The Joyless Open." After the first two rounds, this Open was certainly joyless for Patty Sheehan.

Sports Illustrated continued in its subhead, "Wet weather and Patty Sheehan's collapse marred a tournament won by defending champ Betsy King."

Patty said, "If I had to focus the blame for my Atlanta performance, it wouldn't have been on my motivation."

The course itself was not the problem. Nancy Lopez said it was too short, too easy, the "least intimidating Open course" she had ever played. Louise Suggs, two-time Open champion, said the course was the easiest of any Open course she had ever seen. Louise had seen a lot of Open courses, including the Open track in 1952 at Philadelphia's Bala Golf Club, when Louise won the event, setting a record of 284.

Sports Illustrated quoted Patty at Atlanta as saying, "I like to see an Open course tough. It separates the really good players from the OK players." *Sports Illustrated* quoted her correctly.

The weather in north central Georgia was awful during that Open week. "The most miserable major championship in memory," observed *Sports Illustrated*'s John Garrity. "The three-day forecast: widely scattered golf."

USGA official Judy Bell said, "That Atlanta weather was the worst of any USGA championship in my memory." Judy's USGA memory is long.

It was the Rain Delay Open. On the first day, twenty-seven players were victims of thunderstorm delays and could not finish their rounds. Golf courses are terrible places to be in a thunderstorm. The USGA sounds an eerie siren to let the players and gallery know they're in danger of being barbecued. That siren worked overtime in Duluth.

Patty managed to play in between sirens. The first-round leader board showed Jane Geddes and Patty Sheehan were tied on top with six under par. Nancy Lopez, Cathy Gerring, and Debbie Massey were two strokes back at four under. The temperature was eighty-five that day, with the humidity at a sticky 75 percent. The first round's rain delay was one hour and six minutes.

The second round was rain delayed also—for six hours. Patty teed off at 6:15 P.M. "Good thing the cocktail hour is not important to me," she said.

One can't blame the USGA for being quick with the cease-play siren. In the Men's Open at Hazeltine in Minnesota in 1991, a spectator was struck dead by lightning. Sam Snead had members of his gallery in the Kansas City Open killed by lightning. Sam said, "I don't ever want to smell burning human flesh again!" There was also

a gallery death by lightning at a PGA tournament. "We did not want a repeat of that," said Judy Bell. "So we went out in cars to pick players off the course. A short time later we'd take them back out again. They would play a few holes and then hear another siren. It was hard on the players."

On Saturday during the third round, a six-hour delay in starting was followed by two more shorter delays. Judy Bell kept her cool. "We can play until 8:30 or 8:45. The course is playable." Frantically working crews squeegeed off greens, pumped water out of bunkers.

"You can throw it [the ball] right at the pin," observed ESPN's Rhonda Glenn, as though the rain had been a blessing.

At the end of two rounds, Patty became the first golfer in either the men's or the women's Open ever to reach ten under par at any point in the competition, having shot a 68 to go with her opening 66. She widened the gap between Jane Geddes and herself to six strokes.

And how did Ms. Sheehan occupy her body and mind during the Saturday delay? "I did my laundry and caught up on my book work. The record keeping required for the IRS can get to be too much."

The Peach State had four inches of rain over the tournament's first three days; the drought of the previous four months was over, but the Saturday delay also jammed the final thirty-six holes into Sunday. Why? Why not play eighteen on Sunday and another eighteen Monday?

Judy Bell said the forecast they received from the National Weather Service was for more rain on Monday. "This is a major championship. We cannot shorten it. We elected under the circumstances to play thirty-six holes on Sunday."

Early in the third round on Sunday morning, Patty went to twelve under par and led Betsy King by eleven shots. "But I didn't feel well that Sunday. Doctors told me later that I not only probably had low blood sugar [hypoglycemia] but was also dehydrated. There were two times I thought I would pass out. My legs would simply not move. I had shot the lights out for two rounds and then my game just was not there. I gave nine strokes back to par in the final thirty-three holes."

"[Sheehan] has troubles galore," said TV commentator Dave Marr. "It's going to take a big effort to pull her game together. It would be a terrible thing if she didn't win this tournament. It would take her a long time to get over this deal."

Rhonda Glenn observed that Patty tended to get loose with her swing when she was under pressure. Possibly so. Rhonda Glenn knows golf. So Patty passed that observation along to her pro, Ed Jones, who was busy back home in Reno watching her on television and agonizing because her legs weren't working.

Patty remembers well, "I shot a 35 going out. Then nothing clicked on the back side, morning round. I bogeyed fourteen and sixteen and then chile-dipped my third shot into the water on the last hole. Double bogey seven—and a 75. I still led Betsy King by five strokes."

Ed Jones explained her collapse to anyone who asked by saying, "It's hard to believe, but Patty really doesn't have much stamina."

"Hard to believe? Yeah, I know I look pretty sturdy," Patty commented.

Ask some golf professionals what happened to Sheehan in Duluth, Georgia, that July day in 1990, and a few will clutch at their throats and pretend to gag. The implied word is "choke."

The term "choke" is popularly used in golf to describe a player, or to describe the complex mystery of losing a big lead or failing to pull off a win because of one bad hole. "Choke" implies that the player lacks courage. "Choke" is considered a character defect or a mutation in the genes. Actually, "choke"

—noun or verb—is a complex psycho-physical syndrome.

One LPGA professional, longtime pro Marilynn Smith, suggested to a mutual friend that Sheehan was a candidate for psychiatric help. No one suggested that Arnold Palmer needed a psychiatrist after he gave up nine strokes in the final nine holes to Bill Casper in the 1966 USGA National Open at San Francisco's Olympic Club. Or that Sam Snead needed a shrink when he shot eight on the final hole of the 1939 National Open at Philadelphia Country Club, when a bogey six would have won the tournament. Or how about Ken Venturi's last round 80 that lost him the 1956 Masters by one stroke? Women do not hold the patent on losing big leads or shooting big numbers under pressure.

There is probably no great golfer who has not at one time played like a choke.

The very nature of golf makes lead-losing possible. One bad shot can mean a bogey. One good shot can translate into a birdie. And there you have what the television announcers call "a two-shot swing." All you need to lose an eleven-stroke lead is a few of those two shot swings.

Sports Illustrated reported, "Lunch did nothing for Sheehan's game." Lunch? A sit-down, leisurely, nutritious lunch? No way! The television people were all over her for quotes. She gobbled a turkey sandwich sitting on the bench in front of her locker.

Patty bogeyed nine of the last twenty holes. King birdied the eleventh while Sheehan was in the the process of bogeying the eighth. So suddenly Betsy had a two-shot lead at five under.

The "easiest" golf course had struck back.

But Patty pooled her adrenaline and birdied both numbers fourteen and fifteen. Those birds pulled her back into a tie with Betsy. "Patty has really come back," said Rhonda Glenn. "Patty has the will to win."

"My legs didn't get the message," Patty observed. "Judy Rankin said I had a 'tired swing.'

"My tired swing got to me big time on seventeen. The seventeenth is a 180-yard par 3. Now, legs are useful to stand on when you hit a golf ball, but they need to be used for a lot more than that in the swing. A volunteer gallery marshall yelled 'Stand please!' just as I was setting up for the shot, rupturing my concentration. I made a tired slide into the shot and hit my iron shot into the right front bunker. Under usual circumstances I am a confident sand player, from all those hours spent in Hidden Valley's practice sand trap. But, I had a lot of sand to go over as well as a half-buried lie, and wanting to be sure I didn't leave the ball in the trap, I hit the ball a little thin—didn't take enough sand—leaving myself a twenty-five-foot putt for par."

Patty two-putted for bogey. Now she faced the par-5 eighteenth, on which she had shot a calamitous seven during the morning round. She needed three strokes better than that—a birdie four—to tie Betsy. "I didn't get it."

Her drive was in play, but she half-hit her second shot and then pulled her wedge to the green, leaving herself a twenty-footer to tie Betsy King. She left the putt two feet short.

The most questionable decision Patty made on that long, long, long day was agreeing to a television interview with Judy Rankin right after she stumbled off the eighteenth green. Her blood sugar was probably at an all-time low right then. Her emotional energy couldn't even be seen on the dipstick.

Betsy Rawls, LPGA Hall of Fame member who is now director of the LPGA McDonald's Championship, told a mutual friend, "I would have just kept right on walking." Sheehan should have just kept on walking, right past Judy Rankin, and into the clubhouse. "I think Judy is a great TV analyst, but a lot of people agreed this just wasn't the time for an interview. Judy was just doing her job. I was just doing my job. But the interview should not have been allowed to happen. It was almost as though Judy had said, 'I hear your mother just died. How do you feel about it?'"

When PGA tour stars weep (except for tears of joy or grief like those Ben Crenshaw cried at the 1995 Masters), television refocuses its cameras. Ever eager to prove "Women are too emotional [to play the game]," as telecaster Bob Rosburg once said, the cameras zoom in on any LPGA tears.

So about all the golf world knew about the thirty-eighth USGA Women's Open was that Patty Sheehan blew an eleven-stroke lead, that Betsy King caught her on the eleventh hole of the fourth round, and that Patty had the bad manners to weep on national television. Patty countered that impression by saying, "TV viewers saw that I wasn't the Ice Woman after all. The responses about my crying were very supportive and positive."

Garrity wrote in *Sports Illustrated*, "Better if there had been 40 inches of rain and the whole sorry affair had been washed out."

But that tournament was meant to be. Patty is now grateful for what seemed then a major trauma. "The Open of '90 taught me how to win, how not to put so much pressure on myself. I know now that all the nightmares after that Open—and I literally had nightmares—were not suffered for nothing. Because now I can relax, knowing that I can never again be as disappointed as I was at Atlanta Athletic Club in July of 1990."

As the truism goes, there's no rest for the weary. Patty was committed to play the week after the Open in the Phar-Mor in Youngstown, Ohio. Once a player has committed to playing in an LPGA tournament, only a verifiable illness, injury, or severe personal problem will let her out of the commitment.

Patty recalls her eerie Youngstown experience. "When I walked out onto the practice tee at Squaw Creek Country Club, there was an awful hush. Like walking into a church for a funeral. None of the players would speak to me, because they didn't know what to say. There'd been a death in the family, almost. But my spirit hadn't died. Beth Daniel just barely edged me out to win the tournament. I was runner-up, losing in a play-off to Beth."

Despite her finish in Duluth, 1990 had been a splendid year for Patty. She had won five times, finished runner-up several times, posted her career best scoring average of 70.62—thanks to twenty-nine rounds in the sixties—and paid off the contractor who muscled her Scotts Valley home back onto its foundation after the earthquake. Also in 1990 she became the second LPGA player to top $700,000 in prize money in a single season. (Beth Daniel was the first.) She finished the year as number two on the money list with $732,618 in official cash. Daniel was number one.

Between the National Open of 1990 and the 1991 event, Patty was injured in a freak accident. She was hurt in a part of her anatomy crucial to a golfer—her left hand.

Patty remembers, "It was the evening of the last day of the McDonald's Kids' Classic in Wilmington, Delaware, June 23, 1991. It was at a birthday party for Pam Wright, an LPGA player from Scotland. Pam was celebrating her twenty-seventh, coming up on June 26. Now, this was not a raucous party. The participants might have had a couple of beers or a couple of glasses of wine. Nobody was cutting up or rough-housing."

Many balloons were hanging on the ceiling or bouncing around on the floor. Patty reached for one on the floor. It was a shiny black one that Patty decreed should be back with the other balloons, clumped in a corner of the room. She leaned over to pick it up. Pam, the party honoree, who had been a soccer player, decided she'd play soccer with the balloon, at the same time Patty reached for it. Pam kicked at that balloon as hard as she would have kicked a soccer ball through the goalposts.

But instead of the balloon, she kicked Sheehan's left hand.

"I had a momentary blackout from the pain. It hurt so much I could hardly breathe. I managed to hide my agony. I disappeared from the party for about half an hour to ice my injury. I later learned icing was the best measure I could take on the injury at that point.

"I'm sure Pam didn't kick me on purpose. If she had been trying to disable me she would not have done it there in front of dozens of our friends." Anyone looking for a Tanya-Nancy confrontation will be disappointed. Golf, unlike figure skating, is not a contact sport.

Two days later Patty and manager Rebecca went to the hospital emergency room in Bethesda, Maryland. "Just a bruise," they told her about the now black-and-blue hand.

Patty did not know then, nor did she know for another ten weeks,

that she had fractured a knuckle on her left index finger.

The tournament of the week was a major—the LPGA Championship at Bethesda Country Club, sponsored by Mazda. Mazda also was Patty's personal sponsor at that time. "I could not say, 'I can't play.'" She taped her left index finger to her middle finger, cut two fingers off her golf glove so it would match the taping, and played telling herself all the way "'You cannot finish last. You simply *cannot* finish last.' It would have been better if I'd shot 80–80 and gone on home. Mazda would have forgiven me. I finished in a tie for sixty-fourth place, but I finished!"

Pam Wright made her first LPGA hole in one in that tournament.

What is the psychological attraction of playing with pain? How you play with that pain isn't important. What is important is pinning that purple heart on your chest. It's really a pretty stupid thing to do, because when you're hurt, the flinch in your action that avoids the hurt is going to put a glitch in your swing that's hard to get out.

Back home in Reno, the first doctor Patty went to said, "It won't hurt you to play." But Patty soon learned that playing golf would not help the healing.

In July she played in the National Open at Colonial Country Club in Fort Worth. "The weather was *so-o-o-o* hot! July in mid-Texas? C'mon!" How does the Women's Open always draw July for dates? The only place in the country where the weather is decent in July is on the Pacific Coast, and since the first Open at Spokane Country Club in 1946, the women pros have had only two Opens on the Pacific Coast—in San Diego in 1964 and in Sacramento in 1982. The 1946 Open was not USGA sponsored, however. The Women's Professional Golf Association, predecessor to the Ladies Professional Golf Association, put that one on, with the financial backing of the Spokane Athletic Round Table. Big bucks, they played for—the prize money was $19,000 in war bonds.

Sheehan confesses the confusion shared by many others about how the Women's PGA suddenly turned into the Ladies PGA in 1950. (For details, see the sidebar on page 82.) Call it a Babe Zaharias coup. Babe was declared a professional for appearing in an automobile ad in the late thirties. She regained her amateur standing in the mid-forties and established a fabulous record as an amateur golfer, although not as fabulous as Babe's embellishment made it. Glittering from that record, Babe turned professional in 1947, signed a contract with Wilson Sporting Goods Company and hired as her manager

Fred Corcoran, also manager of stars such as Sam Snead and Ted Williams, and a previous PGA tournament director. Babe glanced at the WPGA's stingy tournament schedule and decided to form a new organization in 1949. The WPGA had by then ceased its corporate existence, so Corcoran's puny excuse that the word "women's" was already taken and that the new organization should thus be called the Ladies Professional Golf Association was invalid. Besides, argued Corcoran, "ladies" had a much nicer connotation. Queen Victoria would have agreed with him.

At the July Open, in Fort Worth, Patty did not distinguish herself. It was getting to be ho hum for her—forgettable National Opens. Despite her injured finger, she made the cut and finished tied for fourteenth.

She then decided to take two weeks off to rest her battered hand before trying to play in the du Maurier Classic in Canada, one of the LPGA's four majors. The other designated majors are the Dinah Shore, the LPGA Championship, and the USGA Women's Open.

For the first time in her career as a professional, Sheehan missed two cuts in a row. That is, she failed to qualify after the first thirty-six holes in two tournaments. Pam Wright finished in a tie for third, not bad for an ex-soccer star.

HOW THE WOMEN PROFESSIONALS BECAME LADIES

A succinct history of the Ladies Professional Golf Association is in *Travels with a Golf Tour Gourmet*. As an introduction to a shrimp and scallops provencale recipe adapted from that served at Fearrington House, eight miles south of Chapel Hill, North Carolina, Betty Hicks wrote:

> *In 1982 I invaded the library of the University of North Carolina at Chapel Hill, intent upon tying together some loose ends dangling from my own files and from my memory about the origins of the Women's Professional Golf Association. The WPGA was predecessor to the current Ladies Professional Golf Association.*
>
> *Our first organization was formed by a transplanted Michigan native, golf professional Hope Seignious (pronounced Sign-nus). The WPGA was incorporated in Greensboro in 1944. Under its auspices Seignious initiated the first National Women's Open (Spokane, Washington) in 1946, and sponsored the second and third opens at Greensboro and Atlantic City, New Jersey, in 1947 and 1948. The winter "tour," initially consisting of a single tournament, the Tampa Open, was another Seignious achievement.*
>
> *But in 1949 Babe and George Zaharias (fearing the WPGA could not offer Babe enough tournaments in which to play) pounced on women's professional golf. "Ladies golf belongs to me!" wrestling promoter George Zaharias decreed. Elbowing Seignious out of the picture, the Zahariases were major factors in the formation of a new organization which Babe's personal manager, Fred Corcoran, quaintly named the "Ladies Professional Golf Association."*

Patty returned home to Reno to see a hand specialist, Dr. Greenwald.

Patty's new manager, Rebecca Gaston, was a radiological technician in her pre-Sheehan life. Becky had actually seen the crack in the knuckle in the first X-rays that were taken, but she couldn't convince the doctor. Dr. Greenwald, with Becky looking over his shoulder, finally saw the break. There was so much inflammation in the joint the first X-rays did not show the fracture clearly.

Corcoran claimed weakly that the name Women's had previously been usurped by a still-existing WPGA. Corcoran was wrong.

"Ladies!" sniffed Hope Seignious indignantly. "'Lady' is what they take out of the inside of a lobster." "Lady" is, in fact, the stomach of a lobster.

Regardless of its crustacean link, the new Ladies Professional Golf Association was incorporated in New York, September 30, 1950. The corporation called the Women's Professional Golf Association had been suspended in North Carolina on December 15, 1949.

But no semantic machinations can alter this fact: Hope Seignious, of Greensboro, North Carolina, founded the women's professional golf tour.

In that rumbling voice which seemed to emanate from the center of his 400-pound body, George Zaharias made his crude philosophy of golf promotion clear. "Golf is a racket, just like boxin' and wrasslin' are rackets. It's gotta be run the same way."

Fortunately for the Ladies Professional Golf Association, while George promoted Babe in his own style, Fred Corcoran was hired by Wilson Sporting Goods Company to promote and schedule tournaments for the LPGA. George Zaharias did not have the opportunity to apply his homespun philosophy to the LPGA. There was enough figurative eye gouging in the LPGA; there was no reason to make that female wrasslin' technique a reality.

Now, six months after her left hand became a soccer ball, Patty had a diagnosis. Dr. Greenwald gave her a syringe full of cortisone in the broken joint. Within two days she was much better. She started physical therapy treatments, and six months after Patty was kicked, she was on her way to recovery.

"The injury was a real downer," Patty admitted. "My broken finger cost me three months of the '91 season. I dropped to number eight on the money list, winning only

$342,204. In spite of the off-year I passed the $3 million mark in tournament earnings."

The forefinger healed with no complications by 1992. Perhaps more importantly, she had healed her mind by 1992. "TV commentator Dave Marr was wrong," Patty explained. "I would get over the National Open disaster in Atlanta. That tournament was just meant to be. No experience ever could be as dismal as Atlanta, 1990. I had nothing to lose."

Sheehan arrived at the forty-seventh annual USGA Women's National Open Championship at Pennsylvania's Oakmont Country Club on a roll. She had won back-to-backs. In late June, with nineteen under, she won the Rochester (New York) International over Nancy Lopez, then the following week she won the Jamie Farr Classic in Toledo, coming from six strokes back.

"One of the most severe tests of golf anywhere in the world" is how *Golf World* magazine described Oakmont Country Club. *Golf World* would not get any argument out of Patty Sheehan.

After Dawn Coe-Jones played a practice round at Oakmont, a club member told her Oakmont was rated the seventh toughest course in the world. Dawn replied, "I am not interested in seeing the first six."

Dawn pretty well expressed the sentiments of all of the professionals. Oakmont had church pew bunkers and greens that said "no way" to players who went for the pins.

"But hey! Oakmont is hallowed ground," Patty said, "and I have respect for the big names out of the past who have won Opens there, Bobby Jones, Tommy Armour, Ben Hogan, Jack Nicklaus, and Johnny Miller."

Sheehan's first two rounds were 69–72, putting her one shot behind longtime friend and former San Jose State University teammate Juli Simpson Inkster. Pam Wright, the soccer player, led the tournament at 139.

But Pam must have gotten kicked in the finger, figuratively, because her wheels started coming off on the front nine of the third round. She eventually finished tied for ninth, with 76–76 the third and fourth rounds.

The closest players to Juli and Patty starting the third round were Donna Andrews and Dawn Coe-Jones, one stroke behind the leaders at 142; Gail Graham at 143; and a few others, the most dangerous of whom were Dottie Mochrie and Meg Mallon, grouped in the mid-

140s. Patty analyzed, "So it kinda came down to Juli and me, a sort of match play format. As an amateur, Juli won a lot of match play tournaments, the biggest being three straight USGA Women's Amateurs. In that tournament you have to win seven matches to be a champion."

On the front nine Saturday, Juli temporarily lost it, pushing her irons into bunkers. But she scrambled to a 37, one over. Juli said on television later that day, "Both Patty and I want so much to win this championship." That was an understatement.

Patty had learned the hard way that wanting a tournament too badly was a great way to lose it. Juli, an admirable competitor, shot eight pars and one bird on the back for a 34 and a 71 total. Sheehan fired a 70 that third round. Inkster and Sheehan were tied at 211 going in to the last round.

On Sunday Juli went out in 33. At day's end she had missed only one fairway and one green. Meanwhile, back at one and two, Patty was bogeying both.

A two-shot swing occurred on the tenth which Patty birdied by snaking* in a 30-footer, while Juli three-putted. On the fifteenth Patty hit her 6-iron up within fifteen feet and knocked in the putt. Back to one stroke behind.

Patty three-putted the sixteenth to drop to two back with two holes to play. In match play Juli would have been described as being "dormie"—as many holes ahead as there were holes to play.

The college teammates both nailed drives on seventeen. The USGA's videotape of the tournament showed an anxious Juli Inkster looking skyward, after she hit her tee shot, toward an ominous black cloud pregnant with precipitation. Déjà vu! That siren—the one that sounded as though its mother had been a World War II air-raid warning and its father a cemetery ghost—sounded.

Rain delay. The twosome escaped to the clubhouse where Sheehan gave herself what she later described as "one helluva tongue lashing. I told myself I'd lost several Opens with cave-ins. It was time I showed I had some guts."

Rainbows always follow rain delays. Brilliant rainbows framed

---

* A snake is a long, sidewinding (due to multiple breaks) putt. It rolls like a snake slithers.

Oakmont when Sheehan and Inkster came back to play one hour and forty-nine minutes later. Play resumed at 7:01 P.M. "As I said at Atlanta, it's a good thing the cocktail hour is not important to me."

On number seventeen, Patty knocked her sand wedge ten feet from the cup and drained it for a birdie. One stroke back; Inkster lipped out for a par from fifteen feet.

On the eighteenth Patty hit her tee shot into rain delay's common product—casual water. This casual water was right in the edge of the rough. Ann Beard, who was head of the USGA Women's Committee, was officiating the Inkster and Sheehan twosome, with USGA President Stuart Bloch looking on. "Ann was going strictly by the book called *The Rules of Golf* when she said that yes, of course I was entitled to a free drop out of the muck. There were some onlookers who accused Ann of favoritism when she allowed me to drop out of the rough. But remember, the rules do not distinguish between fairway and rough. Both these parts of a golf hole are called 'through the green.' Where I had to drop was what the rules describe as 'nearest point of relief.' That means the nearest point that would move my

ball out of the casual water. That nearest point happened to be on the fairway, which wasn't the good fortune it appeared to be, because the drop was onto a downhill lie. Downhills can be tough! But any downhill was better than wet rough!"

Sheehan hit one of the best shots of her golf career after her free drop. She hit a 5-iron, a low screamer that might be expected off a downhill lie. But she hit it pure, right on the stick all the way. The ball stopped eighteen feet from the cup.

The 18-footer was in all the way. Birdie! Juli seemed to be in shock. It was play-off time.

Juli had been in five previous play-offs and had lost only one to Dottie Mochrie in the Dinah in 1992.

Patty had been in ten play-offs and lost six of them.

Based on the record, the odds liked Juli.

Wrong! There's a factor in sports called "momentum." Juli could visualize herself, arms around that big silver Open trophy, hauling it back to Los Altos, California, where it would gleam in the golf shop for all of the members of Los Altos Golf and Country Club to admire. Brian Inkster, the head professional, would stand behind the golf shop counter and beam over his wife's success. Well, the need for a play-off kicked that dream in its solar plexus Sunday evening at Oakmont.

There was one small glitch Patty had to overcome on her way to the play-off Monday. She forgot to bring her golf clubs! Would a psychologist call that repression? She had left them at the private home in which she and Rebecca were living that week. "When we both realized the oversight, I was like Mario Andretti driving back to that house," Patty admits. The great Walter Hagen advised, "Never rush before you play golf." Fortunately for Patty, there was no penalty assessed for noncompliance. The momentum Patty enjoyed carried her into a birdie of the first play-off hole.

Juli's usually reliable putting stroke deserted her. It was Sheehan 35, Inkster 37, on the front. Patty widened her lead to three shots on the tenth. Juli got one back on the eleventh. A birdie on the thirteenth gave Sheehan her three-shot lead back. On fourteen, Juli's putter backfired again. Sheehan now led by four shots.

Patty's reaction: "After Atlanta, I am not sure how much lead I would need to feel comfortable. Maybe fifteen or twenty?"

Sheehan picked up another stroke on sixteen to create a five-stroke margin. But Juli Inkster was not through. Juli and Patty had a history of battles. Juli Simpson Inkster is a competitor. "She never gives up," Patty observed. "You just never know what can happen, like when I was was two strokes down and two to go on Sunday and birdied both holes to tie. I was the one five strokes up and two to go on Monday. But Juli birdied number seventeen and I bogied to shave my lead back to three." At the finishing hole, Juli parred while Patty, drawing a slippery downhill chip from the back of the green, was happy to get down in three.

An incredible tournament play-off was over—Sheehan 72, Inkster 74. After a long and sometimes very painful wait, Patricia Leslie Sheehan was finally the champion of the USGA Women's Open.

Juli's two-year-old daughter Hayley, by then in her mother's arms, said, "Please, Mommy, don't cry." But Mommy deserved that cry. She had had a lock on the National Open, and her good friend Patty impudently grabbed it away from her.

By then Patty was crying, too. "But they were tears of joy, not of the sadness of Atlanta."

The rainbow which followed the rain delay had knocked the monkey off her back.

"They also told us women couldn't break par at Oakmont. I'll argue that one," Patty said. "Juli Inkster and I finished the seventy-two holes in four under."

The 1994 Women's Open of the United States Golf Association was contested at the Old Course of Indianwood Country Club in Lake Orion, Michigan, thirty-five miles north of downtown Detroit. Indianwood had hosted the Women's Open only five years previously, an event won by Betsy King. Scottish professional Wilfred Reid had designed the course to mimic Scottish links land. Reid had installed fescue rough and permitted it to grow to its full, punishing two-foot height. Fescue is a blue-gray ornamental grass that grows in spiky tufts. Hitting out of fescue is comparable to extricating one's ball from a Brillo pad. "Troubles lurked everywhere," commented ESPN's Rhonda Glenn.

The first-round scores didn't look much like fescue trouble. Patty Sheehan shot a 66 along with amateur Carol Semple Thompson and professional Judy Dickinson—and this trio was three strokes back! The Swedish player, Helen Alfredsson, was afire. Her 63 matched the

Open's first-round record. Laura Davies lurked at 68, as did Sally Little and Sherri Steinhauer.

Alfredsson threatened to run away with the tournament. She was ten under at the completion of thirty-six holes, her 132 total setting a record for two rounds. Patty Sheehan knew all about being ten under from her 1990 debacle at Atlanta Athletic Club.

In the third round a potent thunderstorm pummeled the course, causing a two-hour rain delay. Pat Bradley's caddie, failing to compensate for the fifty pounds of golf equipment on his back, tried to jump a low split-rail fence and broke his leg. Laura Davies, who could easily have said to herself, "Jolly-oh! Now Bradley can pack her own sticks," dispatched her brother to finish the round for Pat, a former Open champion.

On the sixth hole of the third round Helen Alfredsson went to twelve under. She followed that with another bird to go to thirteen under, taking a six-stroke lead over second placer Alicia Dibos of Peru. Then Alfredsson started feeling the crunch of Open pressure. She lost a quick four strokes to par as Tammie Green moved to six under. Patty Sheehan snaked one in on sixteen to sneak to within

Patty's culinary talents were allowed an early development in the Sheehan's farmhouse-style Vermont kitchen. At age 3, happily barefooted, Patty whips up some holiday confections.
(Courtesy of Leslie Sheehan)

The Sheehan siblings, poised to attack a Vermont ski slope. Patty was 5, with Steve's protective hand on his baby sister's head, age eight, and Jack and Butch (Robert, Jr.) were 10 and 12, respectively.
(Courtesy of Leslie Sheehan)

Later to develop a singing voice adequate to join the LPGA musical group, "The Unplayable Lies," Patty tuned her young vocal chords by yodeling on a Vermont ski slope.
(Courtesy of Leslie Sheehan)

Getting ready for an upcoming competition, 4-year-old Patty receives some tips from Bobo Sheehan, who coached the 1956 Olympics ski team. Leslie Sheehan, Patty's mother, looks on.
(Courtesy of Leslie Sheehan)

The Sheehan clan at Middle-
bury, Vermont. Left to right:
Patty, 3; Steve, Jack, Butch,
Leslie, and Coach "Bobo"
Sheehan of Middlebury Col-
lege and the 1956 Olympic ski
team renown.
(Courtesy of Leslie Sheehan)

Patricia Leslie Sheehan, 7, enjoyed a fulfilling childhood in a household with three athletic older brothers.
(Courtesy of Leslie Sheehan)

Ten-year-old Patty was now a junior ski champion with six years experience. Patty's golf adventures had yet to extend to the Nevada courses.
(Courtesy of Leslie Sheehan)

"Team" Sheehan prepares to launch. At age 5, Patty had one year of competitive experience, while Steve, Jack, and Butch were winning junior events.
(Courtesy of Leslie Sheehan)

"I've never been much for water sports," admits Patty. Rowboating in the family's back yard pool, dug by Bobo, Patty, and the boys, was the extent of her nautical activities.
(Courtesy of Leslie Sheehan)

As a high school student, Patty worked as a clerk in Bobo Sheehan's Reno ski shop, stocking shelves, doing inventories, waiting on customers, and writing up sales.
(Courtesy of Leslie Sheehan)

Patty was a 17-year-old graduate of Reno, Nevada's Wooster High School in 1974.

(Courtesy of Leslie Sheehan)

Patty, Bobo, and Leslie at the 1978 Women's Open of the United States Golf Association, which took place at the Country Club of Indianapolis.

Oldest brother Steve gallerying Patty in an LPGA tour event. The second golf professional in the Sheehan family, he is a teaching professional in Nevada.

(Courtesy of Leslie Sheehan)

One of Patty's favorite off-tour activities is visiting brother Jack and his family in Middlebury, Vermont, the site of the Sheehan Family Classic benefit golf tournament. Gleeful Patty hoists niece Molly during a 1983 tour respite.

Patty and Bobo at Vail, Colorado in 1983. Patty always considered it a special treat to go skiing with her father. Several years after this photo was taken, Patty chose to go skiing with Bobo in an Olympic reunion ski trip in Switzerland rather than attend the golf tournament of Sarasota, Florida. As a result, the LPGA fined Patty for skipping a tournament as defending champion.
(Courtesy of Leslie Sheehan)

Champagne dousings were to become routine to Patty. This bubbly bath resulted from Patty's 1982 win in the Inamori Classic.

Not one to hide her emotions on the golf course, Patty exhibits jubilation over sinking the winning putt in one of her early tour victories, the 1982 Inamori Classic at the Almaden Golf and Country Club of San Jose, California.

Committee members of the 1982 Inamori Classic helped Patty hoist her oversized check for $22,500. The Inamori Classic was one of Patty's three 1982 wins.

Although Patty came up short for her San Jose University degree by one semester, in 1988, she was awarded an honorary doctorate by Middlebury College. Bobo, Leslie, and proud niece Molly Sheehan attended the ceremony.
(Courtesy of Leslie Sheehan)

Having won the Rochester International for the third time in 1992, Patty shakes up the champagne bottle and splatters the city of Rochester, New York…for the third time.
(Courtesy of Rochester International)

Clan O' Sheehan: the family gathered at Middlebury when "Nanny" Sheehan was only ninety-five. Front row, left to right: Bobo, Nanny, Jack. Back row, left to right: Patty, Butch, Leslie, and Steve.
(Courtesy of Leslie Sheehan)

The young athletes have grown up! Left to right: golf professionals Butch and Patty, and amateurs Jack and Steve. This was the first time the four siblings had ever played golf together. They played the day before Patty left for the 1993 LPGA tournament in Stratton, Vermont.
(Courtesy of Leslie Sheehan)

As the 1993 Rochester International champion, Patty Sheehan takes dead aim. *(Courtesy of Rochester International)*

Patty's custom Nevada license plate proudly announces her presence in the LPGA Hall of Fame. *(Courtesy of Cheryl Traendly)*

Patty prefers digging dirt in her verdant Nevada garden to diggin' dirt about her sister LPGA members. *(Courtesy of Cheryl Traendly)*

PATTY SHEEHAN
PROFESSIONAL GOLFER   1992

Women golfers have finally arrived in the sports world! They're now featured on sports collector's cards. This particular one presents professional golfer Patty Sheehan with 29 wins in 1992 (one short of the LPGA Hall of Fame requirement).

Patty aligns a putt in the 1995 Rochester International. *(Courtesy of Rochester International)*

Patty and *Patty Sheehan on Golf* co-author, Betty Hicks, celebrate Betty's 75th birthday in Cupertino, California, November of 1995. Patty and manager Rebecca Gaston surprised Betty by flying from Reno for the occasion. Patty and Betty are longtime friends, first meeting in 1972.
(Courtesy of Betty Hicks)

Patty and her manager, Rebecca Gaston, are sitting in their four-acre backyard of "Chateau la Tour," the home they share in Reno, Nevada.

Having inspired and molded Patty's golf swing since she was thirteen, Edgar Jones, Patty says, is the number two leading man in her life. Ed was a longtime head professional at Reno's Hidden Valley Country Club. He was also a World War II bomber pilot and a former PGA tour player.
(Courtesy of Cheryl Traendly)

"Chateau la Tour," Patty's 6,000-square-foot home was inspired by a French farmhouse. However, her extensive lawnmowing duty does have its drawbacks.
(Courtesy of Cheryl Traendly)

In addition to gardening, Patty's domestic pleasures extend to cooking. In her sprawling kitchen, she delights in creating new dishes.
(Courtesy of Cheryl Traendly)

Callaway Golf makes it eminently clear that Hall of Famer Patty Sheehan plays their equipment. Patty has signed a contract with Callaway, receiving an amount equal to the royalties of any of their male staffers.

(Courtesy of Callaway Golf)

three of the lead. Then Helen lost two more with bogies on sixteen and seventeen.

Helen Alfredsson shot a third-round 76. That figure coincidentally matched Patty Sheehan's third round at the Atlanta Athletic Club in 1990.

Meanwhile, Patty Sheehan was enjoying her own round. She said to herself, "Maybe I should make this putt [on the seventeenth] to take the lead." She did, causing Rhonda Glenn to comment to the network watchers, "Who can catch Patty Sheehan?"

But Patty just felt she was one of a big pack. "I didn't feel any pressure of leading the Open." Patty showed signs of cracking, however, in the fourth round when she drew a bad bunker lie at the ninth and left a shot in the sand. *Golf World* described the shot as a "nasty downhill lie." When Sheehan leaves one in a bunker, you know the lie was nasty.

Patty was tied at six under with Tammie Green, but then Green left a birdie putt short on number fifteen. Always dangerous Lisolotte Neuman moved up to third; Alicia Dibos took over fourth place.

The sixteenth was the critical hole. Tammie Green hit her drive into a fairway bunker. Her weak out left her ball in the rough. Patty also hit her drive into the rough, but her recovery left her only four feet from the hole. She holed the putt for a birdie and the tournament lead.

Seemingly unable to resist fescue's lure, Patty again hit her tee shot into the Scottish links rough, but again hit the green from her off-fairway location. Tammie hit her second fifteen feet away on eighteen, but as thousands watched on television, she missed the putt to the right.

Sheehan was left with a 4-footer for her second open win. The putt was a left-to-right breaker. "Not my favorite. It was also a downhiller. I just thought, 'All right, I've hit thousands of these in practice; just do the same now.'" She drilled it into the heart of the cup for a 277 and a new U.S. Open record.

"I knew by Friday I had a lot of golf left in me," grinned Patricia. "I was more relaxed. And I'm so happy to win on Sunday, rather than going to Monday as I did in 1992."

Caddie Carl Laib won Patty's first hug, father Bobo her second. The prioritizing was due to proximity, not length and intensity of the relationship with either man. Then Patty did a run around the gallery, an exuberance patented by Hale Irwin after his Open win in 1990. She slapped any extended palm she could reach. "Now *that* was fun!"

Was it diplomatic immunity that exonerated Sweden's Helen Alfredsson from media charges of choking, from sister professionals' hints that she needed psychiatric aid to pull her through the crisis of collapse? (Helen shot 76–77 in the final two rounds.) *Golf World* writer Pete McDaniel insightfully summarized Patty Sheehan's recovery from her 1990 calamity and Alfredsson's comparable disaster.

"[Patty] provided the latest—though not necessarily the last—proof that she has put the Atlanta nightmare and all her other U.S. Open nightmares, comfortably behind her.

"'I learned there's a lot more to life,' said Sheehan of her post-1990 recovery, 'than losing the U.S. Open.'

"Now Alfredsson, as talented as any twentysomething on the LPGA Tour, finds herself facing the same hard lesson.

"Is Sheehan's return amazing?" McDaniel asked, then answered.

"You bet. Golf's history is full of the sad accounts of players who suffered stupefying collapses in major championships from which they never recovered. Sam Snead lost the 1939 U.S. Open by triple-bogeying the 72nd hole. Arnold Palmer coughed up a seven-shot lead in the final nine holes of the 1966 Open. Ed Sneed lost three shots on the last three holes of the 1979 Masters. Bobby Clampett led the 1982 British Open by five shots after 36 holes before staggering home a loser. Each player, in one way or another, was never the same.

"But not Sheehan. Someday when this outgoing, fun-loving, high-stepping goofball hangs up her knickers and retires to that dream house she's built in Reno, Nevada, it won't be her thirty-four-plus victories, her $4 million-plus earnings, or even her corner in the LPGA Hall of Fame for which she'll be most remembered. It will be for the fact that she choked away the U.S. Open at the age of thirty-three, and then came back to win it. Twice."

Could it be that the words ski coach-father Bobo Sheehan uttered twenty years before on a snowy Sierra slope stuck with her through the decades? When Patty caught a ski on a starting gate and was tempted to give up the race, Bobo commanded, "Boot it!" That's ski talk for "Get going!"

And "Boot it!" Patty Sheehan did.

FAIRWAY WOODS

Ed says, "The problem most of us have is trying to help the ball up. The ladies are probably a little more guilty of this than the guys. "

It's for sure I didn't try to help the ball up when I double-eagled that par-5 seventeen at Rochester in 1989. Using a 3-wood, my second shot found its way to the cup. Ed is a great believer in keeping golf and golf instruction simple.

I can add something, though. Real aids in this era of high-tech clubs are the very high-lofted metal fairway woods which are available now. Oh, sure, the manufacturers have long produced clubs in complete sets of woods—numbers 1 through 13. But the trouble was the lofted clubs cut back too much into the necks of the old wooden clubs. They weren't as strong as they should have been and cracked too easily, especially the persimmon woods. Clubs made of persimmon wood had great feel, but the persimmon absorbed mois-

High-lofted wood clubs by Callaway. These are the clubs you'll need the most on the fairway.

FAIRWAY WOODS
continued

ture and then dried out, leading to cracking. We don't have that problem with metal woods.

Particularly if you're a woman beginner, remember that *loft is your friend!* I see my women pro-am partners trying to get the ball into the air from the fairway with 2-woods. As a sage, old clubmaker used to say, "Golf is tough enough; don't handicap yourself with your equipment."

Use no less than a 4-wood from the fairway. Depending upon your skill level, a 5-wood may be even better. If you have a driver, put it away. Use your 3-wood to drive with. You'll get more distance off the tee if you get the ball into the air.

SHOTS FROM THE FRINGE

Ed and I were sitting around the lounge at Hidden Valley, reminiscing.

"I'll never forget how I won my first tournament, the one in Japan, by sinking a putt from the fringe on the last hole."

I hold down the club several inches. (I am using a pitching wedge here.) I stand with my feet close together, hands slightly ahead.
© *Cheryl Traendly*

I use my hands a lot on these shots with a little automatic response in my arms. I neither try to keep my body still nor force it to move. Notice that my hands do not pass the clubhead as I go through the ball (4). That's an important basic. Many higher handicappers try to scoop the ball up, disregarding the fact that the loft of the club will do that for them. Result: "fat" or topped shots.

© Cheryl Traendly

SHOTS FROM THE FRINGE
continued

Ed responded, "That gives me a good opening to talk about shots from the fringe. You've got a whole bunch of clubs in the bag that'll do the job for you. It depends upon the individual doing the chipping. Like ol' Muffin Face, Bobby Locke, the great one from South Africa who ripped us up in the '40s and '50s. Every time he needed some money he'd come over here and play a few tournaments, get out his wedge and chipped it from every place, including an inch off the green. History tells us he was very successful at it. He used the wedge exclusively.

"On the other hand, Greg Norman won the World Series of Golf with a 7-iron chip-in. You've got a whole bagful that can do the job. You just have to take them and work with them, to find out which ones you have the most confidence in."

For techniques from the fringe, see photos on previous two pages. There are two basic methods of hitting chips: with hands and wrists working, and with hands and wrists locked in place. I prefer to use my hands and wrists. I get a better feel that way. But suit yourself. There are some very good chippers who lock their wrists out of the chip. The captions for the photos describe my techniques for you.

FAIRWAY BUNKERS

"Remember, Ed, that bunker shot I hit in Phoenix on the thirteenth hole on the final day? I hit a wood out and caught the top of the bunker?"

Ed grimaced. "I sure do. You were trailing Dawn Coe-Jones by one stroke. And when she knocked it up three feet for a possible

On a good lie (ball sitting up in the sand) from a shallow fairway bunker, the only modifications I make are at address. I try to set up so I take no sand behind the ball. I bore my feet into the sand for stability (1). I play the ball back (to the right) in my stance more than I would for a fairway shot with a wood (2). Then I take a normal swing and let nature take its course (3–6).

© Cheryl Traendly

FAIRWAY BUNKERS
continued

bird, and you left your third shot in a greenside bunker, I thought 'Goodbye, Hall of Fame.'"

"Then I holed out from the greenside bunker and Dawn missed her putt. All of a sudden, there I was with a one-stroke lead instead of being three strokes back."

You gotta get some breaks to win golf tournaments. You have to have the techniques to take advantage of the breaks, too.

"So much depends upon the lie you have in a fairway bunker," Ed contributes. "We don't want to get sand between the face of the club and the ball. This may require a little adjustment in your stance; play the ball a little farther back. It's important you have the confidence that you can swing the club and let it do the job for you."

In retrospect, I might have done better with that fairway bunker shot if I had used a more lofted club. Average players should *never* use a wood from a fairway bunker, no matter how good the lie, no matter how shallow the bunker.

SIDEHILL LIES

Although golf is a game of great integrity, golf is not played on the level. There are uphill lies, downhill lies, sidehill lies with the ball above the feet, sidehill lies with the ball below the feet, and innumerable combinations of those. Refer to page 115 for a summary chart of sidehill lies which may clarify this complex subject somewhat for you.

The most famous sidehill shot I ever hit was a downhill 5-iron on the seventy-second hole of the 1992 Women's National Open at Oakmont, following a free drop from casual water. I hit a low screamer, to be expected from a downhill lie, which was on the flagstick all the way. The putt I had remaining was an 18-footer, which I sank to tie Juli Inkster and force a play-off. I won the play-off the next day.

DOWNHILL LIES

Take one or more clubs longer on a downhill lie. How much more or less club to use depends upon the severity of the slope. I can't give you a formula for it.

Ed advised me that on uphill and downhill lies, play the ball more opposite the high side of your stance. To state the advice another way, play the ball more opposite your uphill foot. "Of course, it depends upon the severity of the situation," Ed added, "how much uphill you need to play the ball." On an uphill lie, play the ball more opposite your left foot than you would normally play it.

Allow your weight to go to your downhill foot. Let your weight go in the direction gravity is pulling you. On a downhill shot this means play the ball nearer your right foot.

Then be careful to follow the contour of the slope with your swing. That is, on a downhill shot, follow the slope *up* with the backswing and *down* with the follow-through.

On a downhill lie, the likelihood of pushing the ball exists. I'll aim a little bit left on the downhill shot. The push isn't guaranteed to come off, though. It's just a good possibility.

I try to swing a little straighter back and through on these side-hills. Swinging straighter back and through produces less body turn, making it easier to maintain balance.

UPHILL LIES

On an uphill lie, most of the modifications are just reversed from that of a downhill lie.

SIDEHILL LIES
continued

The memory device "ball uphill, weight downhill" still applies. That is, the ball will be played more opposite your uphill foot— your left foot. Your weight will go in the direction gravity is pulling you—toward your right foot. Hit a longer club than normal for the distance remaining.

Allow for a possible pull by aligning more to the right. Please don't take my name in vain if you aim right on an uphill lie, hit the ball on the toe, and go right!

Again I try to swing straight back and straight through, minimizing the body turn produced, to help maintain balance. Follow the contour of the slope with your swing: down with the backswing and up with the follow-through. On very severe uphill slopes with a

Downhill

Uphill

SIDEHILL LIE SUMMARY

Lie	Stance/Swing Adjustments	Possible Ball flight
Downhill	Ball Uphill Weight downhill. Follow the slope with your swing. (Up with the backswing, down with the follow-through.)	Push. Lower than normal flight. Use more loft than normal.
Uphill	Ball Uphill Weight downhill. Follow the slope with your swing. (down with the backswing, up with the follow-through.)	Pull. Higher than normal flight. Use less loft than normal.
Sidehill, ball below feet	Bend knees more Bend over more from waist Swing as straight back and straight through as possible.	Push. Allow for push by aligning several yards left of target.
Sidehill, ball above feet	Hold down on club two or three inches Straighten knees slightly Swing as straight back and straight through as possible.	Pull. Allow for pull by aligning several yards right of target.

© Cheryl Traendly

Sidehill, ball above feet   Sidehill, ball below feet

SIDEHILL LIES
continued

short swing, you may have to allow your left elbow to bend on the follow-through so you can follow the slope up. This is especially true if your uphill lie is on the face of a sand bunker. If you bang into the face of that bunker, you could hurt yourself!

BALL ABOVE THE FEET

Play the ball stance center. Grip down on the club several inches. You may want to straighten your knees a little. Distribute your weight evenly, from the balls of your feet to your heels. Align a bit right to allow for a possible pull. Swing straight back and straight through, with a shorter than normal swing. You'll need a longer club for the distance, due to the shorter swing.

Hey, did I say these sidehills are easy? Some sidehills are so severe you almost have to consider you've knocked your ball into a hazard and take your penalty stroke. But most are playable. A little bit of practice on sidehills can produce good returns in skill and confidence.

FEET ABOVE THE BALL

When your feet are above the ball, you'll have to bend your knees a little more to get down to the ball. You might also need to bend more from the hips. Grip the club on the end. Play the ball stance center.

The lie encourages a pushed shot. Aim left—and hope you don't hit the ball on the toe!

Swing straight back and straight through, using a shorter swing than you normally would. The shorter swing necessitates using a longer club for the distance remaining. Depending upon how high your feet are above the ball, you may take as little as a half swing.

A good way to practice sidehills is to find a hill from which you can hit short shots and, with your wedge or 9-iron, hit a variety of sidehill lie shots of between twenty-five and fifty yards. You won't have the balance problems with a short shot and can better practice stance modifications and following the contour of the slope with your swing. Drilling on these shots will also help you with the problem of remembering all of the modifications.

CHAPTER FIVE

THE HALL OF FAME

On March 21, 1993, there were twelve members of the Ladies Professional Golf Association Hall of Fame. They were not there as a result of a popularity vote, though entrance to many sports halls is decided by a vote of the fans or media representatives. All had earned their right to dwell there. "It's the proverbial eye of the needle," wrote the *Los Angeles Times'* Jim Murray, "for entrance into golf's kingdom of heaven."

Patty Berg, Betty Jameson, Louise Suggs, and Babe Zaharias were the first inductees in 1951, but under criteria different from today's. "How in the world," many observers ask, "did Betty Jameson, with only ten pro tournament wins, get into the hall?" How, indeed? Well, the Women's Golf Hall of Fame, established in 1950 in Augusta, Georgia, had seven electors, three of whom were amateurs. Twice national amateur champion in 1939 and 1940 (in which there

were no Open Championships) and Open champion in 1947, Jameson was a constant contender on the LPGA tour, coming off a magnificent amateur record. The original Hall electors did not limit their review to a golfer's professional record. Betty Jameson's amateur record was exemplary. Her professional record was not one for which Betty owed any apologies.

Though the standards were different, when the LPGA established its own Hall of Fame in 1967, it voted to "grandmother" the original residents into its new sanctum sanctorum.

No one joined the original foursome until 1960 when Texan Betsy Rawls, who was to win fifty-five tournaments in her career, met the criteria established by an LPGA membership with little foresight. But what crystal ball could have visualized Title IX dumping scores of talented young women players out of the colleges and onto what

119

had been a thirty-player roster of contenders and near-contenders in the 1950s and the 1960s?

The membership decreed in 1967 that an LPGA member of ten consecutive years of good standing could gain residence in the Hall by winning thirty official LPGA tournaments, including two *different* championships decreed as majors. The tournaments anointed as majors were the Dinah Shore, the LPGA Championship, the USGA Open, and eventually the du Maurier Classic of Canada. Or a member could qualify by winning thirty-five tournaments with one major among them. That's how Nancy Lopez became a Hall of Famer. She had won the LPGA Championship three times, but sorry, Nancy, it only counts as one. Nancy had to win thirty-five tournaments with only one major. An alternative route was to win forty times, none of them a major.

Strange as it seems in Nancy's case, allowing more than one victory in the same major championship was rejected by the LPGA. Win the USGA Women's Open six times? Sorry, count it as only one major. Unless one was an intimate witness to the thought processes of the LPGA membership in the 1960s, such odd reasoning is inexplicable.

Mickey Wright, arguably the greatest woman golfer of all time,

was permitted entrance to the original Hall in 1964. Mickey was destined to set a record of eighty-two victories before her early retirement after thirteen years on the LPGA tour. Eleven years would pass before another star, who eclipsed Mickey's record with eighty-eight tournaments, more than any man or woman professional ever claimed, placed the name of Kathy Whitworth in the hallowed Hall.

Sandra Haynie joined the elite group in 1977, as did Carol Mann. Sandra and Carol were to go on to forty-two and thirty-eight career triumphs, respectively.

Five years later, JoAnne Carner became eligible. Big Mama Carner was to put away forty-two titles. Another five years passed until Nancy Lopez became number eleven in the Hall. However, the LPGA tripped over its own ten-year membership requirement and, with a red face, had to ask Nancy, despite her forty-seven tournament wins, to wait at the door for a few months until she had been an LPGA member for the required number of years.

Pat Bradley, with a fistful of majors, won her thirtieth in 1991 and became number twelve in the Hall.

"If they don't change the criteria, there will be nobody in the Hall of Fame but a bunch of old ladies," was Patty Sheehan's cryptic observation. "And soon they'll die off and there won't be anybody alive in there and the whole thing will be obsolete."

The specter of a pile of cadavers, each of the deceased wearing spiked shoes, is the creation of Patty's macabre prediction.

Opinions of LPGA players and officials differ on changing the entrance requirements. "Leave 'em like they are," declares JoAnne Carner. JoAnne is a member of the committee which has spent several years reviewing the criteria.

"I made a commitment to get into the Hall of Fame that took nineteen years to accomplish," says Pat Bradley. She believes younger players should make that same commitment. She also believes the Rolex Player-of-the-Year and Vare Trophy awards should count in the point totals, as do several other honors.

"I don't want to get in and have an asterisk after my name," protests Beth Daniel, who yearns to be inducted according to present criteria. No one has argued that winning several of the same major should not count as one major. There is consensus on one factor: winning tournaments on the LPGA tour today, with 300 players on the roster, is an infinitely greater challenge than winning

tournaments when there were only thirty players.

Consider this fact: In the 1950s the fledging LPGA had to lower itself to its organizational knees and beg its thirty-some players to enter each event, so they could collectively be called a "field." Only a handful had any illusion they were entering tournaments except as members of the chorus line. The championships were all won by players named Rawls, Suggs, Zaharias, and Berg, with an occasional impudent appearance by Jameson, Hanson, Pung, or Hagge, with a sometimes upstart amateur, a Polly Riley or a Pat O'Sullivan, vaulting atop the leader board.

For the record, in 1948 three players—Berg, Jameson, and Zaharias—won all of the seven tournaments on the schedule. Five years later the LPGA had been an organization for three years, and there were twenty-four tournaments with seven different winners. Louise Suggs won eight events.

Today the LPGA field is closed at 144 players, most of these competitively hardened young athletes, who come directly to the LPGA out of college programs. Count the winners for 1994 as an example: there were twenty-four winners for the thirty-five events on the tour. Only one player, Beth Daniel, won four tournaments. Lisolotte Neumann and Laura Davies won three each. Little wonder the media challenges the LPGA to change its nearly impossible entrance requirements. Little wonder a committee appears to be in constant session.

"Yes, we're working on it," insists Debbie Massey, player representative on the committee. The assignment of the committee is to rewrite the entrance requirements in an acceptable form.

Writing in late March of 1993, Jim Murray observed in his *Los Angeles Times* column, "The women get no break at all. You know how many players there are in their Hall of Fame? Thirteen. A baker's dozen.

"Know how many guys are in baseball's Hall of Fame?" asked Murray. "Care to guess? Two hundred and fifteen. And the Pro Football Hall of Fame requires the election of at least five every year. Even if, say, two of them don't get the required number of votes. They go in on the coattails.

"Thirty tournaments is a nearly impossible yardstick, given today's hotly competitive tour. It's like requiring a batter to hit .400 every year—or at least for two years—or to have a lifetime average in the .350s or to drive in 200 runs. A football player would have to throw or catch 50 touchdowns in a year, sack the quarterback 20 times a game, or run for 3,000 yards a season.

"Take the case of Patty Sheehan. She probably has the best golf swing seen on any tour since the young Gene Littler. She had won 29 tournaments up to this year—only 17 male golfers have won that many—including a U.S. Open and two LPGAs. She has won $3,591,290 (fourth-highest total in women's history) on the tour.

"But is this Hall of Fame stuff? Nope." Not just yet might have been a better answer.

Patty began her inexorable march into the LPGA Hall of Fame in 1981 when she won her first LPGA event, the Mazda Japan Classic. In 1982 she added three more victories—Orlando, SAFECO, Inamori. In 1983 she upped the number to four for a total of eight—Corning, LPGA Championship (a major), Henredon, and Inamori. Patty dittoed the number in 1984 with the Elizabeth Arden, a second LPGA Championship, McDonald's, and Henredon. She annexed only two in 1985—the Sarasota Classic and the J and B Scotch pro-am. After only five years on the LPGA tour, Patricia Leslie Sheehan had one foot in the Hall with a total of fourteen tournament wins including one major.

In 1986 she notched three more wins. Then in 1987 Patty slipped back a step in her quest for a seat in the Hall; she inexplicably experienced her only winless year on tour.

"I didn't realize I hadn't won until next year when people started to tell me I hadn't won that year," she remembers.

There were, of course, explanations. "I was having some personal problems. People who were meaningful to me—people on the LPGA tour, fellow competitors—were telling me I wasn't a very good person. They were giving me a lot of very negative input. So I didn't feel very good about myself. The main reason I didn't play very well is that I had stopped believing in myself. I went through therapy with a psychologist; the therapy taught me a lot about myself. I wasn't sure who I was, what kind of person I was, what was important. I learned I did have self worth. As soon as I got over feeling bad about myself and not liking myself very much, I started to play better. In 1988 I started to win again."

That year she added two victories. In 1989 she chalked up one, the Rochester International. In 1990, striving to pay off huge bills to repair the damage done to her home by the October 1989 earthquake, a motivated Patty won five events—Jamaica, McDonald's, Rochester, Ping-Cellular One, and SAFECO. She won another in 1991, the Orix Hawaiian.

In 1992, Patty brought her victory total to twenty-nine, including a second major, the U.S. Open. She became the first woman to acquire the double crown when she won the British Open, in the autumn of 1992, to parlay with her U.S. Open win that year, but this victory failed to tally in the eyes of LPGA rule makers. The British Open was deemed an "unofficial event."

"To me," declared Patty, teeth clenched, "the British Open is a major."

Patty's manager, Rebecca Gaston, had buttons made for Patty's fans announcing, "The Hall Calls." The Hall did, loudly.

On March 22, 1993, Patty Sheehan and Dawn Coe-Jones led the Standard Register Ping Classic at fourteen under par, teeing off in the fourth round at Phoenix's Moon Valley Country Club. Coe-Jones grabbed the lead when Patty three-putted from ten feet on the third hole, but Patty knocked in an 18-footer for a birdie on nine to take back the top spot on the leader board.

Coe-Jones played the back nine with two bogeys and no birdies, and had to watch her playing partner birdie the eleventh and thirteenth. Patty gave one back with a bogey on fifteen, but she still nursed a four-stroke lead going into number eighteen. "I didn't feel really comfortable all day until I knocked it close on number 18 for that birdie putt. It was not a very good ball-striking round. I was pretty nervous all day."

Her final 70 was good for a total of 275, seventeen under par and a tournament record for seventy-two holes at Moon Valley. A third-round 65 had positioned Patricia to make her move to triumph number thirty. She won by five strokes. In only thirteen years on the LPGA tour, Patty Sheehan had swung her way into the LPGA Hall of Fame. Zero to thirty in thirteen years—the fastest entrance ever made into the hall.

The champagne corks klooped. (Don't you *love* that sound, Patty?) That word *is* in any unabridged dictionary: "kloop," sound of a cork coming out of a bottle. Kloop, kloop, fizz, fizz. Patricia Leslie Sheehan, the LPGA's thirteenth entry into the Hall of Fame, became a bubble collection center. Friends aimed the sparkling liquid at the Mazda logos at point blank range, thumbs jamming the opening in the bottles' necks to increase the velocity of the emerging bubbly.

They could not miss. Neither could LPGA Commissioner Charlie Meachem with a bouquet of thirty red roses.

Juli Inkster wept joyful tears for her ex-college teammate.

"Hey," Patty cautioned Juli, "I'm the one supposed to be doing the crying." Juli's answer was to erupt in spasms of sobs.

"I'm happy to get it over with, happy to be in the Hall of Fame," grinned Patty, now also $105,000 richer. "I'm glad not to have to think about it anymore. It's been quite a burden."

Five hundred friends and admirers gathered in the grand ballroom of the Reno Hilton Hotel on November 13, 1993, witnesses to Patty Sheehan's formal induction as player number thirteen into the LPGA's Hall of Fame.

None but a handful of the 500 had ever seen Patty Sheehan in a dress.

She made a memorable moment even more memorable by the gown she had selected, a sequined dazzler in turquoise with a coy amount of Patty's stingy cleavage showing and a sizable divot out of the back. With laudatory premonition, she had bought the dress in a Naples, Florida, shop one month before she won her thirtieth tournament.

The LPGA orchestrated the evening magnificently. Theme Sheehan was everywhere. Silhouettes of Patty's trademark knickers adorned an exhibit of Patty's achievements. Separate banquet tables seating eight guests each were decorated with golf flagsticks numbered thirteen.

Profiles of Patty's elegant follow-through were featured on small banners at every table. Souvenir wine glasses, commemorating "Patty Sheehan's LPGA Hall of Fame Induction, November 13, 1993" were take-home treasures. A gargantuan banner behind the speaker's podium saluted number thirteen.

At each place setting was a green-bowed miniature scroll of the LPGA Hall of Fame Proclamation:

WHEREAS Patty Sheehan has been a member in good standing of the Ladies Professional Golf Association since 1980, and

WHEREAS she has demonstrated her outstanding golfing ability as evidenced by her career victories—including four major championships—and further evidenced by her Rookie-of-the-Year, Rolex Player-of-the-Year and Vare Trophy honor; and

WHEREAS she has continued to perform outstanding service to the Association and to women's golf.

NOW THEREFORE, on behalf of the membership of the Ladies Professional Golf Association we attest and officially recognize the induction of Patty Sheehan to membership in the LPGA Hall of Fame in which she entered on the 13th day of November, 1993

Commissioner Charles S. Mechem, Jr.
November 13, 1993.

LPGA tour players, Hall of Famers, and Hall of Fame aspirants, stiff in their facial makeup, teetering precariously on unaccustomed high heels, provided an effusion of mirth to the preinduction ceremonies. Beth Daniel was prominent among them, no doubt being asked by tactless well-wishers when she planned to join the Hall.

Joanna Kerns, onetime star of television's "Growing Pains" and sister of Olympic swim star Donna de Varona and golf professional Kurt de Varona, was the mistress of ceremonies. On her podium was mounted a miniature pair of knickers.

Patty's turquoise gown glittered as she mounted the speaker's stand to accept her first award of the evening, a Kachina doll Eagle Dancer from the Phoenix Standard Register Ping Classic. The Kachina was handmade by Henry Shelton.

"I wish I'd had Eagle Dancer on October 17, 1989," sighed Patty, referring to the devastating California Loma Prieta earthquake of that date, which had moved her spacious home off its foundation.

Joanna next introduced Patty's manager, Rebecca Gaston, a former radiological technician and medical equipment saleswoman whose friendship with Patty was initiated when Rebecca asked for Sheehan's autograph at an Ohio LPGA event in 1982.

An obviously nervous Becky stumbled over her lines as she recounted life with Patty Sheehan. "In addition to the champagne, there have been a lot of diet Cokes along the way. Clairol," suggested Rebecca, "should introduce a new hair color called LPGA Alabaster White." The reference was to the thirty-eight-year-old Sheehan's rapidly graying hair. "I thought of commissioning a bronze bust of Patty," added Becky, "but I rejected that as inappropriate. Patty Sheehan is not a bust, even though on at least one occasion her career was classified as over. So I commissioned sculptor Tom Bennett to do a full bronze of Patty." And with that she unveiled the dramatic two-foot statue of Sheehan in her renown follow-through.

Patty, for the only time in the evening, was near speechless. "Wow!" was all she could say. The statue was a total surprise, an unleaked secret. "I am in shock." Patty turned a complete 360 degrees on the platform, searching for words. She found none.

The awards continued to mount in rapid succession. Juli Inkster, on behalf of Patty's tour peers, declared Patty "a great friend, a great person." But because Juli charged Patty was also a "cartoon character," the LPGA sought the talents of the organization's long-time friend, Charles Schulz, to depict Patty with Snoopy as her caddie. "We love her!" Juli declared simply as she presented the framed work by the renowned cartoonist of Peanuts.

"Snoopy does kinda look like Carl," quipped Patty, obviously enjoying the evening more and more with each new astonishment.

Patty's only complaint during the night of revelry concerned the condition of her residence in Reno's Lakeridge community. "I don't appreciate the TP all over my house," said Patty in mock seriousness. "And I don't appreciate the chalk outlines of dead bodies in the street in front of my house, particularly since one was wearing knickers."

Caroline Keggi was the artist who admitted culpability along with Meg Mallon, who in 1993 won two majors (the LPGA Championship and the National Open) in a stretch of three weeks. The model around which the chalk was manipulated was Connie Wilson.

Six of the eleven living Hall of Fame members were at Patty's party.

PAVING THE ROAD TO THE HALL

Patty Sheehan set a new record as she entered the LPGA Hall of Fame. With two separate major championships in her victory list, Patty entered the Hall more rapidly than any of the other twelve residents. After her first win in the Mazda Japan Classic in 1981, Patty's moving van arrived at the Hall entrance after a journey of only twelve years. In those twelve years on the LPGA tour, Patricia Leslie Sheehan collected these titles. (Majors are shown in bold face.)

1981	Mazda Japan Classic	1988	Sarasota Classic
1982	Orlando Lady Classic		Mazda Japan Classic
	Safeco Classic	1989	Rochester Invitational
	Inamori Classic	1990	Jamaica Classic
1983	Corning Classic		McDonald's
	LPGA Championship		Championship
	Henredon Classic		Rochester Invitational
	Inamori Classic		Ping Cellular One
1984	Elizabeth Arden Classic		Safeco Classic
	LPGA Championship	1991	Orix Hawaiian Open
	McDonald's Kids' Classic	1992	Rochester International
	Henredon Classic		Jamie Farr Toledo Classic
1985	Sarasota Classic		**U.S. Women's Open**
	J & B Scotch Pro-Am	1993	Standard Register Ping
1986	Sarasota Classic		Entered the LPGA Hall of
	Kyocera Inamori Classic		Fame as a result of her
	Konica San Jose Classic		thirtieth victory in the
1987	(No wins)		Standard Register Ping.

In addition to the above tournaments Patty has also won:

1992	British Women's Open
	(declared an unofficial event by the LPGA)
1993	**Mazda LPGA Championship**
1994	LPGA Skins Game (unofficial)
	U.S. Women's Open
1995	Rochester International
	SAFECO Classic

Each was allotted a place on the program to laud Patricia.

Kathy Whitworth has won more golf championships than any player, male or female. At one time the golf world asked, "Can Kathy do it? Can Kathy Whitworth beat Mickey Wright's record of eight-two tournament wins?" Kathy did it by a resounding six.

"A marvelous occasion. A great party, Patty!" Kathy said of the celebration. "Patty fought being a superstar," the all-time winningest one observed. "I am glad to see her become—for Patty's sake—the great player I knew she could be."

Louise Suggs followed. "Patty has been screaming about the Hall being nothing but a bunch of old ladies. Did you hear the one about the time Patty visited a nursing home? She spotted an old lady sitting in a corner, walked up to her and said, 'Do you know who I am?' 'No,' replied the LOL, 'but if you'd go out to the front desk, I'll bet they can tell you.'"

Betsy Rawls, the fifth golfer inducted into the Hall, was introduced by Joanna Kerns, as "a true winner in every sense." Betsy, director of the McDonald's Kids' Classic (now the McDonald's LPGA Championship), recalled how Patty had been scheduled for a promotional appearance in Wilmington, Delaware, early on the Monday following the LPGA championship. Then Patty won the LPGA, contested in Bethesda, Maryland. "Uh, oh," said Betsy to herself, "there goes our promotion. Patty will be too busy celebrating."

But Patty, on two hours' sleep, drove from Bethesda to Wilmington to honor her commitment. "She was her usual enthusiastic, warm self," reported Betsy, "and she did the promotion for no money. I am proud to add my congratulations to Patty."

Carol Mann, 1977 inductee to the Hall, exulted, "I love watching you play golf, Patty. I love watching you swing a golf club. Please don't stop playing. I recognize that you have gone through your own struggles, the internal things you have gone through. We all need support. You have chosen your support team well: your parents, your brothers, Rebecca Gaston. You can't do it by yourself."

The inductee to precede Patty Sheehan into the Hall was Pat Bradley, who entered in 1991. "I'm just happy," said a relieved Pat, "that I don't have to follow Patty Berg as a speaker. We all knew it would come—Patty Sheehan's entrance into the Hall of Fame. She has those essential qualities: commitment, perseverance, desire, courage, talent—and a sense of humor."

That other Patty, Patricia Jane Berg, whose years of stardom extended from 1938 into the 1970s, who devours joke books in preparation for her many public speaking appearances, initiated her evening's performance with, "I'm going to start with a coupla stories. They're old, but so am I." Patricia Jane Berg was not old; she was seventy-five at the time of Patty Sheehan's induction. "This guy said to his friend, 'I just got a new set of golf clubs for my wife.' The second guy said, 'Good trade!'

"Hank Aaron, former star of the Atlanta Braves, claims it took him seventeen years in the majors to reach 3,000 hits—and he did it in one day on the golf course," Patty reported in her distinctive, staccato style of speaking. "And another great ball player, George Brett, said he shot three over—one over the clubhouse, one over the front patio, and one over the swimming pool.

On a serious chord, Patricia Jane Berg, who had acquired fifty-seven wins in her tour years, an astounding fifteen of those majors, made her tribute to Patricia Leslie Sheehan. "Patty Sheehan is a great champion. She is a wonderful representative of the highest standards of the LPGA. You have proven to be a great humanitarian, Patty Sheehan. God love you. God bless you always."

A representative for Rolex watches, Rick Bannerot, was introduced next. Obviously in jest, he reported that Patty Sheehan, owner of several Rolexes awarded for various honors, had enough Rolex watches. So Patty called to the podium Mom and Dad, Leslie and Bobo. Both were awarded gold Rolexes. "Anybody want to buy my old Timex?" asked Bobo, tossing his bargain watch on the table, proving the sense of humor was in the Sheehan genes.

"Although Patty Sheehan has earned several Rolexes," said Rick, "she does not have a dress Rolex." A grinning Patty extended her left arm, wrist exposed, and received another Rolex.

Joanna Kerns, admitting to an "overwhelming feeling about the LPGA," introduced Commissioner Charlie Meachem Jr., who initiated his presentation by reading a letter from George Bush to Patty Sheehan. Bush's father, Prescott, was onetime president of the United States Golf Association.

"Patty Sheehan," intoned Meachem, "is in a category that transcends all others. Some get there by the magnificence of their talent—as Mickey Wright. However a player arrives in the Hall of Fame, she breathes rarified air.

"Patty Sheehan stands out most in the fact that she has never done anything unprofessional. She is the consummate professional. Sometimes she is nuts," smiled Meachem. "Sometimes she is vain. Sometimes she is off the wall. But she always does what she needs to do at the time she needs to do it. She is always a credit to the LPGA, to women's golf, and to herself.

"One of the penalties of being inducted into the Hall of Fame," the commissioner went on, "is that you have to endure a poem written by the commissioner."

Bring Forth the Echoes

A mighty year it's been all right,
And a mighty one afore it.
Patty made the Hall of Fame,
And all golf's better for it.

She always was a fightin' lass,
And showed it o'er and o'er.
But, 'twas at Oakmont's fearsome
playing field,
That she notched her greatest
score!
Aye, and while she fought that
monster course,
And ghosts and demons ran,
'Twas heard a wee small voice, an
echo like-
Ye can Sheehan, ye can, ye can.

It then came down to
just one more,
To enter our great Hall of Fame.

Phoenix was the time and place,
Moon Valley was the game.

For those poor few who
wondered whether,
Miss S. could beat the ban,
That same still voice echoed
yet again,
Sheehan she can, she can, she can!

The rest is history as they say,
Yet one feeling's with us still.
Our love for this superb performer,
Has not dimmed—and never will.

And so, the final whisper—
the last echo,
comes from every Sheehan fan,
Can we love ye little lass,
We can Sheehan, we can!! we can!!

Charlie Meachem added, "I don't know what I would have done if her name were Kowalski."

The honoree was then introduced. "How do you like my dress?" was Patty's opener.

The cheers and whistles and applause were deafening. When they died down, Patricia Leslie Sheehan set about thanking all of the people who had helped propel her into the LPGA's Hall of Fame.

Patty initiated her acceptance speech with a good-news/bad-news story.

"The good news is that I have tested negative for triskadekaphobia. I do *not* have an unnatural fear of the number thirteen. The bad news is that I can't remember how to spell Atlanta.

"I had heard early in my golf career that this Hall of Fame was the toughest in all of sports to get into," she began before remembering her first professional teacher, Dud Phinney of Middlebury, Vermont. "Dud Phinney charged twenty-five cents a lesson then, and he still charges twenty-five cents a lesson.

"Then in 1969 we joined Hidden Valley Country Club, here in Reno. I started taking lessons from Ed Jones, Hidden Valley's professional. And I soon learned that when I was on the practice tee and was having trouble with my swing, all I had to do was talk into that little intercom on the tee and say to Ed in the golf shop, 'Ed, you got five minutes?' Ed always had five minutes, and five minutes was all it took Ed to patch up my swing.

"Betty Hicks was teaching a summer course in golf at the University in 1972 and she came to Hidden Valley for a golf clinic. She looked at my old Ben Hogan clubs and decided they weren't doing much for me. So she sent me a new set of Wilsons; she worked for Wilson Sporting Goods Company in golf promotion. I didn't feel good about playing with illegal clubs, but I didn't feel bad enough not to beat other amateurs playing illegal clubs.*

"I always got more out of golf instruction from real people, not from books, but one time I was going to our state high school championship in Las Vegas and I saw this golf book at a store in the mall and I thought I might learn something on the bus ride to Vegas. I sure did! The book was named *The Happy Hooker*. Boy, was I a naive teenager!"

Patty continued with her appreciations. "Someone to whom I am most grateful for my golf career is Juli Inkster. When we were both at San Jose State University, I asked Juli one day, 'Do you think I could make it as a golf pro on tour?'

"Juli answered, 'What else are you going to do with your life?'

"Even if I don't remember how to spell it, the Open in Atlanta was very important in helping me win the tournament in 1992. Even though I became infamous for losing a big lead in Atlanta, that tournament taught me how to win.

"The most memorable single moment I've ever had walking

---

*The USGA's rules of amateur status are very rigid. Amateur golfers cannot accept expense money. Amateur golfers are also forbidden by USGA rules to accept free equipment, but except for the wealthy few who can afford their own equipment, most amateurs accepted clubs, balls, and shoes.

down a fairway—even more memorable than the British Open, was the last day at the Standard Register Ping in Phoenix. It was an unbelievable rush, hearing that applause when I knocked my second shot on number eighteen stiff for a bird, knowing all of those people admired me, loved me.

"The rush I felt walking down the eighteenth at Moon Valley was from the feeling that I had done as well as I could do. The pressure on me to get into the Hall of Fame was finally coming to an end."

For so long Patty had expected so much of herself. She was hard on herself. "I was never completely happy with the way I putted or the way I hit the ball. It was a marvelously warm, loving feeling that I received from the crowd and from the players, not only those I was playing with, but those who stood nearby on the final green.

"Finally I had done something that very, very few players had ever done. The feeling was both of accomplishment and relief. I felt relief from the pressure of not having to look back and say "I could have putted better," or "I could have hit the ball better." My only thought was, "Now I'm in a place where not many people are. The journey to get into the Hall of Fame was finally over. Just now I'm going to be a sponge and absorb all of the cheers and congratulations.""

"I've got to thank Dud Phinney, because he taught me discipline when I was still a single-digit age.

"But Ed Jones is the guy who had to put up with my teenage temper. Can there be any human activity which is both as rewarding and as frustrating as the game of golf? Ed Jones, through his teaching genius, taught me the simplicity of the golf swing, taught me the excellent fundamentals that have brought me here tonight.

"The caddie-player relationship involves a teamwork which is unparalleled in sport. Carl Laib, if you can still stand after all of those years of carrying my golf bag, please do so."

Laib (pronounced Lie-b) stood proudly. Carl knew he had done his job well.

Patty then named all of the others who had preceded Carl as her caddies. She thanked her personal sponsors, who trusted her to promote and market their products—*Golf for Women* magazine, Taylormade golf clubs, Neumann golf gloves, and Mazda of America.

There were others to thank. "To my dogs Sherlock and Quincey. They love me no matter what I shoot.

"For six and one half years, Rebecca Gaston has helped ease the logistical burdens of the tour, helped me regain my sense of self-worth, wiped away the tears, poured champagne over my head, helped me grow. Like Sherlock and Quincey, her love has been unconditional.

"My three brothers, Butch, Jack, and Steve, obnoxious as they could be at times, taught me about athletics, taught me how to compete. . . .

"All of my life, my parents gave me guidance, discipline, courage, morals, integrity, honesty, self-worth, and a sense of humor.

"They also gave me $4,000 to start on the tour, regarding it as a tax write-off. But when I started making money, the tax was too much, so we had to dissolve the partnership. Mom and Dad, when you say you love me, I don't have to say 'Prove it!'

"Everyone here tonight means something to me—from my childhood, my adolescence, my career."

Charles Meachem then directed toasts to Patty. As the glasses were raised, Patty Sheehan threw kisses to the crowd. And when the audience whistled, Patty Sheehan characteristically stuck her fingers in her mouth and whistled back.

GREENSIDE BUNKERS

Ask me to recall my most memorable shot, and next to that 3-wood I holed for a double eagle at Rochester, New York, the bunker shot I holed at Phoenix's Moon Valley Country Club en route to my thirtieth win and the LPGA Hall of Fame has to be runner-up. That holed bunker shot was the tournament's turning point. With a one-stroke lead, Dawn Coe-Jones had hit her second shot three feet from the cup for an almost—but not quite—certain birdie on the thirteenth hole. I'd half-hit a fairway bunker shot and then left my third shot in a greenside sand bunker. I was hitting my fourth shot; Dawn was hitting her third. The probability was that she'd take a two-shot lead with only five holes to play.

Please know that by this time in my golf career I had hit so many practice shots out of sand that it was second nature to me. But you might want to check *your* hows against *my* hows to improve your sand shots, so here's the technique for a ball sitting up in the bunker:

GREENSIDE BUNKERS
continued

I play the ball slightly left of center. Weight is evenly distributed. I have bored my feet into the sand for stability. The clubface is slightly open.

I have an early wrist set. I don't like the term "wrist cock." It implies violence. I like "flex" or "set" better. Notice my wrists are completely flexed at the completion of the half swing. Notice also that even though I am only hitting about a thirty-yard shot here I've taken almost a full swing.

Now, it appears in the sixth photo of this series that I am pulling down with my left. A lot of instructors teach, "Pull down with your left." That advice is simply too easy to overdo. "Pull down with your left" is dangerous. It's a great way to shank it!

In the seventh photo, it's obvious that the swinging clubhead has caught up to my hands. The clubhead has slid into the sand. The sand has moved the ball out of the bunker; the clubhead has not. My advice to you is this: just feel that you are taking a shallow divot out of the sand. Practice—and we hope your home club has that valuable learning area, a practice bunker—just taking shallow divots out of the sand, without hitting balls.

In the sequence's eighth photo, note that my right hand is turning over my left and my head is beginning to rotate into the finish.

Opposite:
Top left: The ball is sitting atop the sand in a greenside bunker. I play the ball slightly left of center. My weight is evenly distributed. I have bored my feet into the sand for stability. The clubface is slightly open.

Top right: I have an early wrist set.

Bottom left: Notice my wrists are completely flexed at the completion of the half swing.

Bottom right: Even though I am only hitting a thirty-yard shot here, I've taken almost a full swing.

© Cheryl Traendly

Opposite:

Top left: It appears in this photograph that I am pulling down with my left hand. And some instructors teach, "Pull down with your left." But it can be dangerous advice because it can easily be overdone. It's a great way to shank it!

Top right: The swinging clubhead has caught up with my hands and has slid into the sand. It is the sand, not the clubhead, that has moved the ball out of the bunker. Just feel that you are taking a shallow divot out of the sand.

Bottom left: My right hand is turning over my left, and my head is beginning to rotate into the finish. My right heel has come out of the sand to permit me to turn into the follow-through.

Bottom right: This is a cardinal rule on bunker shots: your follow-through must be as long as your backswing. Think of your target on your follow-

through—where your hands will be on the finish—before you even start your backswing. On most shots, I say the follow-through is the result of club-head velocity, but on bunker shots the sand will slow the club down after impact if you allow it to.

Above left: The reason golfers may leave a ball in the bunker is that they hit too much sand as a result of quitting on the downswing. Think follow-through.

Above right: On a buried lie, you are confronting an almost totally different challenge because you've got to move a lot of sand. To move the ball out, you must swing the clubhead all the way under the ball. The modifications I make at address are: ball centered, hands slightly ahead of the ball, and weight slightly more on the left foot. We are trying to produce a downswing shot here.

© Cheryl Traendly

GREENSIDE BUNKERS
continued

No head down for this pro! My right heel has come out of the sand to permit me to turn into the follow-through.

This is a cardinal rule on bunker shots: your follow-through must be as long as your backswing. Think of your target on your follow-through—where your hands will be on the finish—before you even start your backswing. Balls stay in the bunker because too much sand is hit as a result of quitting on the downswing. *Think follow-through!*

On a buried lie in a bunker, you are confronting an almost totally different challenge because you've got to move a lot of sand. The

Again I have used a quick wrist set. A quick set is all the more important with a buried lie because you need a vertical arc.

© Cheryl Traendly

138

modifications I make at address position are these: Ball centered. Hands slightly ahead of the ball. Weight slightly more on the left foot. We are trying to produce a *downswing* shot here.

Again, just as on the top-of-the-sand lie, I use a quick wrist set.

Notice how much more sand I have taken with the buried lie than with the good lie. I have gone all the way under the ball to hit it out, so I've used a very vertical "angle of attack," as Ed Jones, bomber pilot, would call it.

Notice how much more sand I have taken with the buried lie than with the good lie. I have gone all the way under the ball to hit it out.
© Cheryl Traendly

ROUGHING IT

"Shots out of the rough are kinda like snowflakes," said Ed Jones. "No two are exactly alike."

Height of the grass is an obvious variable. Rough is not going to be the same length at Muleshoe Muni as it is at a USGA tournament.

Type of grass is another very important variable. Indianwood Country Club's fescue is one miserable example at the far end of the

In advance of a shot from the rough, you have to picture the ball bouncing off the clubface at the same angle as the angle of the clubface. This is because you have to give the ball a trajectory which will clear the rough ahead of its position of address.

Photo by Cheryl Traendly

Because I am hitting a pitching wedge here, I have a more narrow stance than normal. My hands are an inch or two ahead of the ball at address, promoting a downward blow on it.

Photo by Cheryl Traendly

You can't even see the ball in the rough here, so notice I am using plenty of loft—a high-lofted wedge.

Photo by Cheryl Traendly

An abrupt "pick-up" or wrist flexion is essential on this shot. A low, sweeping backswing is just not going to get the job done because you will have too much grass between the clubhead and the ball. You can't "mow that much hay" and still have enough clubhead velocity remaining when you reach the ball.

Photo by Cheryl Traendly

scale. And bermuda can jump up and grab your club; you can bend a wrist tendon or two in that stuff. Wet rye is the same way; this grass can wrap around your clubhead like a boa constrictor.

"It reminds me of a line some clever sportswriter came up with during the Masters one year," said Ed Jones. "The guys were grinding the leading edges of their wedges so they'd cut through the

ROUGHING IT
continued

rough better. 'Sharpest wedges ever honed' was how the writer described them, paraphrasing the Gillette razor ads of the day."

The advantage gained by the loft of a sand wedge is not adequate to counteract the disadvantage of that big sole tangling with the grass. You're better off with your highest-lofted pitching wedge.

You have to picture the ball bouncing off the clubface at pretty much the same angle as the clubface angle.

You have to have a very good lie in the rough to use a wood out. This is especially so for the higher-handicap players. The basic rule is to get safely out of what we once called "Euwell Gibbons country." (Several decades ago Euwell Gibbons was a famous naturalist-explorer type.)

As far as alterations in swing techniques in rough are concerned, there is an important one. *Use a more abrupt, or quicker, wrist break on the backswing.* This is especially necessary on short shots out of the rough around the greens, when your swing is so short you can't generate enough clubhead speed to overcome the resistance of the long grass. You just have to avoid as much of the grass as you can, as shown on page 143.

A bit firmer grip than normal will also help prevent the grasping grass from twisting the clubhead in your hands.

Naturally, the stronger you are, the better your recovery shots from the rough will be, all other variables being equal. Put yourself on a good weight training program for golf.

One of the best exercises is to take a bucket of range balls out to a challenging length of the uncut and hit them out.

The line drawn between the club-head and the ball here shows the abrupt angle on the downswing resulting from an early wrist set on the backswing. If there is any secret to shots from the rough it is this wrist flexion or set.

© Cheryl Traendly

The follow-through is a result, not a cause. It results from the velocity of the club through the ball. The follow-through is not created as an after-thought. It is not artificially tacked onto the end of the swing.

© Cheryl Traendly

THE PITCH SHOT

"What's the weakest part of Patty Sheehan's game?" a reporter asked Ed Jones.

"Sure, she's had some putting problems lately," Ed replied, "but I'd call it a phase. The weakest part of Patricia's game is her wedge shot. She has a tendency to drive the ball in, rather than tossing it. I don't know what to do about the weakness other than getting her to trust the loft of the club."

"Aw, Ed, you know I love to drill it in there, have it bounce once, and then check up."

Ed shrugged, "How are you going to argue with a Hall of Famer?"

"Easy," I answered, "just argue. Tell me about my wedges."

"Watching you in Palm Springs as I do every year I've seen that club cost you, kiddo. Someday maybe you'll have to say, 'Well, I'm going to get some versatility and I'm going to learn to toss that ball in there where the situation calls for it.'"

I grinned, "OK, but other than that, how's my game?"

Ed grinned back, "Pretty solid. Pretty solid."

The best wedge tips I've ever heard come from a variety of sources, like my putting tips I've collected.

"Set it and leave it." That's from Joe Davis, who was a pro at Spartanburg Country Club, Betsy Rawls' home course. What Joe meant, in his stingy southern way of expressing himself, was to break your wrists immediately away from the ball and leave them cocked until impact with the ball.

Now, there are pros such as Ed Oldfield, who has worked with Jan Stephenson and Betsy King, among others, who believe in a theory promoted by Ken Venturi—lock your wrists on the wedge shot. Whatever works for you is right for you. My problem with this stiff-wristed swing is that it is not versatile enough. You can't use it out of rough. You can't use it out of bunkers. I like one swing that can be used for a great variety of shots, and that one swing requires a wrist set at the start of the backswing.

"Swing it like you're swinging a bucketful of water." That's from Harvey Penick. And it's valuable advice because it is "feel-based." Swinging the bucket of water gives you rhythm and the tempo so important on the wedge.

"Clip the dandelion." This is another "feel" drill. You have to feel the lowest part of your swing arc, and clipping dandelions is a good way to do it.

"Like you're using a weed cutter." This came from the revered old professional, Victor East, and was further promoted by Harvey Penick. I personally use a hoe to chop weeds, but that's not going to work here. And if I use a weed cutter in my garden, I'm going to have stumps where my corn stalks were. The weed cutter is good, but I prefer the bucket-of-water drill. The choice is yours.

"Keep the backswing and follow-through the same length." We hear so much about the follow-through that some golfers, particularly the women who like to follow instructions to the letter, tack artificial follow-throughs onto their swings. The result: deceleration on the downswing. In addition they're probably trying to follow-through with their heads down. No way!

Strangely enough, if you try to imagine you're hitting against an obstacle on the downswing—an obstacle which is the same distance as your backswing—you'll accelerate the club through the ball. Acceleration through the ball is useful in error avoidance. I'm thinking particularly of fat shots here. Golfers who "chunk" it (hit behind the ball) on wedges have usually slowed down on the downswing. No amount of looking at the ball will rectify that.

Acceleration also increases backspin. I discuss the subject of backspin on page 180. Avoid trying to accelerate consciously. The same length backswing and follow-through will take care of that for you.

Remember, corrections that can be overdone are hazardous to your golf game's health.

CHAPTER SIX

PATTY SHEEHAN: HUMANITARIAN

"Patty couldn't have been more than thirteen," remembered Leslie Sheehan. "She'd just gotten her learner's permit to drive. She was driving on a country road just outside Reno when she saw a dead bird beside the road. She stopped the car, got out, and ever so tenderly, carried the bird into a nearby field, scooped out a shallow grave with a broken tree branch, and buried the little critter.

"Patty has always, in spite of her tough competitive exterior, had a tender heart."

Thousands of dollars have poured out of Patty Sheehan's heart during her golf career.

Her most publicized charity, although Patty certainly did not request that it be so, was Tigh Sheehan in Santa Cruz, California. "Tigh" (pronounced tee) means "house" in Gaelic. House of Sheehan.

Barry McDermott, writing in *Sports Illustrated* in March of 1984, extolled Patty's athletic talents. "But there is another side to Sheehan," McDermott wrote. "Few athletes are more generous with their love, their time and their money. Sheehan is a soft touch. Need help? See Patty. She donated $3,000 to an LPGA tournament in San Jose. Can't get your life together? Talk to Sheehan."

Tigh Sheehan was not established with the goal of putting Patty's picture on the cover of *Sports Illustrated* or eliciting an invitation to a state dinner at the White House. Tigh Sheehan was conceived because there were adolescent girls in Santa Cruz County who were emotionally wounded; they needed Patty Sheehan's help.

In the early 1980s, Margaret Leonard, a California attorney who had played for the University of Santa Clara golf team when Patty played for San Jose, was Patty's business manager. Margaret's mother, Anne Leonard, created the Group Home Society, opened the front door on Halloran Hall, a residence for disturbed and neglected young-sters in Aptos, California, and later opened a girls-only home, Giuliani Independence Hall, in Soquel. Television star Merv Griffin was her supporter. Merv, a tennis addict, conducted an annual celebrity tennis tournament on the Monterey peninsula to raise money for the Group Home Society.

"Merv was marvelous," Anne remembers admiringly. "He never forgot names—the dog's name, the girls' names, the counselors' names. He'd even visit the home and call the kids' friends. 'Hi, this is Merv Griffin,' he'd say, and the recipient of the call would inevitably say 'You've got to be kidding!' He was not kidding."

Merv Griffin's celebrity tennis tournament became an overwhelming organizational project, and Merv eventually withdrew his support after several marvelous years of contributions to Group Home Society.

So Anne Leonard turned to Patty Sheehan for financial assistance.

, "The girls need a pool table," Anne said of the residents of Giuliani.

Patty responded without hesitation. "A done deal."

"And," Anne began hesitantly, "the girls need more housing facilities."

"The girls" to whom Anne referred were strikingly like Anne in her own youth. Anne Leonard, orphaned at age nine, was raised by an aunt in the small Michigan town of Hart. Anne met John Leonard in Marquette, Michigan. They raised a family of stalwart athletes: two boys (Joe and Jim, the latter an outstanding football lineman for the San Francisco Forty-Niners, the San Diego Chargers, and the Oakland Invaders of the USFL), and Margaret, the golf star. Even before the conception of Group Home Society, Anne and John Leonard had long offered one of their spare bedrooms to any child with emotional or physical abuse problems.

"More housing facilities," Patty mused. Her own childhood was the antithesis of those of the troubled youngsters for whom Anne Leonard pleaded.

"I'm getting eight to ten referrals a week," said Anne. "Youngsters abused or neglected by their families, with no place to turn. One girl was homeless—on the streets at seven years old, stealing to buy food. The mother of another gave her to the police, to gain God's redemption. We have many with eating disorders—anorexics and bulimics. The first year's expense for an additional home would be around $25,000."

Patty Sheehan, memories of her own incomparable childhood scrolling before her eyes, quickly responded, "Let's do it." She took out a $120,000 mortgage and spent another $10,000 to remodel the house that had become the newest Group Home Society's facility.

The home, in a residential neighborhood in Santa Cruz, was a two-story, four-bedroom, white-frame house whose inhabitants ranged from thirteen to seventeen in age. They lived with their adult counselor. All of the adolescents had experienced family traumas: alcoholic parents, drug-using mothers or fathers, child abuse. Some had no parents. Some came directly from the Stanford University clinic for emotionally disturbed youngsters. "According to the California Youth Authority," said Anne Leonard, "we had the highest success rate of any group home in the state."

A poster of Patty Sheehan, prominent in the living room, was hung at the insistence of the original residents.

"Patty's very good with the kids," said Anne Leonard. "Maybe it's because she's a kid herself. I think Patty's so involved with this project because she didn't meet these kinds of kids when she was growing up. She was at the top of her class at Wooster High School, she is an athlete, and she comes from a great family."

"Tigh Sheehan really opened my eyes," Patty admitted. "I'd had such a Polyanna upbringing. I'd only heard about abuse. I had never seen the damage. Some of those girls were so badly damaged we could only try to help them; there was really no hope."

Tigh Sheehan housed up to six adolescent girls at one time. "What strikes me when I first meet one of them," says Patty, "is how little they have, and how much even minute things mean to them."

The minute things were abundant. Sheehan collected cast-off clothing from other LPGA tourists. Sportswear companies contributed quantities of last year's styles. Patty saved the amenities from the hotel rooms where she stayed on tour and carried bagfuls of shampoos, soaps, shower caps, and hand lotions back to Tigh Sheehan. "Here I am, with about everything, and they're with nothing, and yet we feel close to one another. We chat about common goals. You know, the ol' life, liberty, and pursuit of happiness stuff."

Lucy Wilbur, a social worker and therapist who worked with the girls, observed that the association of the girls so used to losing with a real winner was therapeutic.

Anne Leonard observed that Patty had a lot of talent working with teenagers. The girls were not even aware of her status as a golf champion. They just liked Patty for

Patty. And she was particularly influential in job training and job placement. Patty, knowing adolescents need incentives to stay in line, came up with a scheme to keep the youngsters working at their summer jobs. The previous dropout rate had been 100 percent.

"Work at a job all summer," Patty challenged, "save two-thirds of your money, and I'll send all of you to Disneyland who do that." Twelve of the residents of Group Home Society's three houses earned trips to Disneyland the first year of the program. Patty gleefully paid the air fares and bills at the Disneyland Hotel for these kids who had never seen an airport or been on an airplane. The program continued for eight years, at one time inspiring thirteen youngsters to meet the Sheehan challenge.

Charles Kuralt sent four cameramen from New York to produce a television special on Tigh Sheehan starring Patty. The set was ready-made; the house was a decorator's dream. A Santa Cruz furniture dealer had donated the services of his interior decorator. Furniture maker Henredon, sponsor of an LPGA tournament in North Carolina, challenged Patty. "Win this tournament again, Patty," said the furniture manufacturer after Sheehan's 1983 victory, "and I'll completely furnish Tigh Sheehan." The 1984 Henredon was won by Patty Sheehan. The furniture manufacturers sent eleven catalogs for Patty, Anne Leonard, and their decorator to choose from. "Tigh Sheehan should have been in *House Beautiful*," was Anne's appraisal of the stunning results.

How the youngsters got to Tigh Sheehan, whether they wandered in off the street or were sent there from juvenile hall, didn't matter to Anne. The critical theme in their lives was that they were separated from their parents; they had no family. "The separation issue was big for these girls. Now we were that family," said Anne.

Patty Sheehan was very much a part of that family, visiting Tigh Sheehan as often as her rigorous tour schedule would permit, on an average of once every eight to ten weeks. "Commander in chief of this teenage Salvation Army," Barry McDermott, writing in *Sports Illustrated*, called Patty.

"They need someone to look up to," Patty admitted. "It's great to be that person, even though I don't see myself as anybody special. But they do. That's what they need and I'm willing to give it to them."

Nobody special? In the early 1980s Patty was still fighting off the greatness of her golf career, still not foreseeing her entrance into the Hall of Fame, her two LPGA championships, her two National Open wins, her Player-of-the-Year, her Vare Trophy, her Rolex watches for top this and best that.

Patty had no images of the Charlie Bartlett Award in mind when she established Tigh Sheehan. She had no dreams of being on the front cover of *Sports Illustrated* as one of the eight Sportsmen and Sportwomen of the Year. "I'm kinda shocked," said Patty when she was informed of the awards. "The girls and their counselors and house parents deserve more recognition. They put in a lot more work than I did."

Marino Parascenzo, president of the Golf Writers of America, presented the Charlie Bartlett Award in memory of the beloved Charlie, longtime golf writer for the *Chicago Tribune*. Parascenzo stated the Bartlett Award was only given in years they found "someone we consider worthy of it." When Patty won the accolade in 1987, it had not been awarded since 1984. She was the second woman recipient; the other was Patty Berg, who won for her work on behalf of the American Cancer Society.

"I wanted to to something I had a special feeling about," Patty told Tampa sportswriter Tom McEwen. "Sure, I could have just written out a check to a charity, but the extent of my involvement would be very limited. I wanted to contribute to something I could see and touch. I go by Tigh Sheehan and they cook me a meal. We'll have our annual Christmas party there soon.

"Y'see," continued Patty, "I don't feel that what I do—play golf—while I love it, is, well, going to change history. It doesn't help the Ethiopians get a square meal. It's not a space walk like Dr. Kathryn Sullivan did. Kathryn Sullivan comes to mind because I had the honor of having a state dinner with her and others with President Ronald Reagan recently. I got the invitation blind in the mail. *Sports Illustrated* had selected the Sportswomen and Sportsmen of the Year—athletes chosen for their humanitarian work. What a thrill!

"It was scary, going to the White House, even though they sent an escort to pick me up. Here came this handsome guy in his dress uniform. I think, but I can't be sure, that he was in the Coast Guard."

In the morning, the group of honorees went into the White House Rose Garden for speeches and gun salutes. At dinner time they adjourned into a small room near the entrance to the house.

"The Duchess of Luxembourg was there, and Bryant Gumbel and

Floyd Patterson and Dr. Sullivan. It was great. President Reagan told a couple of Russian jokes.

"But, on a scale of one to 10, golf is maybe a one in overall contribution. Oh, I know it means I can do other things because I play and earn money and it is entertaining and an economic force. It's just, well, not that big to me in the overall scheme of things. My golf game is not going to change the world."

Tigh Sheehan may not have changed the world, but the home changed the lives for many of its residents, and that's what that $125,000 mortgage was all about. And that's why the selection panel at *Sports Illustrated* chose Patty Sheehan specifically for her work at Tigh Sheehan.

Patty continued her involvement with Tigh Sheehan from 1982 until the 1989 Loma Prieta earthquake forced Patty to move back to Reno, Nevada. Patty, a hands-on humanitarian, did not feel she should continue her association with Tigh Sheehan if she could not be there.

The media was also an issue. Patty doubted how much she was helping these troubled kids when her notoriety robbed them of their privacy, their right to continue their growing-up process without having the media constantly intruding to do stories about them.

When Patty's liaison with Tigh Sheehan ended, she turned her efforts in other directions. Soon the headline in the Reno newspaper shouted:

Thanks, Patty!
You're helping women at UNR

Many might have argued that Patty Sheehan had little reason to donate her time and energies to the first of her two alma maters. Doubtless a money crunch affected the University of Nevada's treatment of Patty when she was a student athlete there, but UNR's athletic department could have been a bit more respectful of the young woman who was obviously a present and future star. Unless forced to do so by local outcry or government intervention, most male-dominated athletic departments do little or nothing for women's programs.

"Can you chaperone Patty to the tournament in Hawaii?" (or Albuquerque or wherever) was not an unreasonable request for a fund-strapped school; UNR athletic administrators asked this author frequently. (Chaperoning Patty was always a pleasure, up to but not including the night in Albuquerque when she let the air out of all four tires of the Tulsa University's team station wagon.)

However, during Patty's enrollment, UNR launched no fund raising for the women's golf team and made no attempt to build a team around Patty. But Patty's loyalty streak was so deep that the simple location of the Reno campus to her new residence, her three-year attendance there, along with her mother's prior affiliation as a professor of nursing, was adequate to prompt her into fund-raising action.

Under their headline of gratitude, the Reno daily explained Patty's new involvement with her alma mater, "With women's athletic programs at the University of Nevada-Reno under extreme financial pressure, it's gratifying to see a former resident of the community and national sports figure donate her time to benefit the school.

"Professional golfer Patty Sheehan, leading money winner on this year's LPGA tour, is scheduled to be the center of attention today at Hidden Valley Country Club. She will stage a short clinic, play nine holes with various amateur partners and host a barbecue—all to benefit women's intercollegiate sports programs at the university.

"Her national image could easily demand a substantial fee for such an appearance. Other athletes demand—and get—big money for speaking engagements and personal appearances even though they rarely need it. But here's a genuine case of the unselfish athlete."

Patty had other projects as well. In the early 1970s, an LPGA teaching professional, once a contestant on the women's professional tour, Joanne Winter of Scottsdale, Arizona, was teaching hordes of kids at a Phoenix driving range, Cudia Park. "And I thought to myself, watching these talented kids swing at a golf ball," remembered Joanne, LPGA Teacher of the Year in 1969, "where are they going to display their skills here in Arizona? We had a state championship and an invitational. That was it. They need more competitive opportunities."

Originally, Joanne planned to sponsor a coeducational youth tournament, with a girls' division and a boys' division. Then she decided that a girls-only event would be enough of an organizational challenge.

All golf tournaments, from the smallest club championship to the National Open, have price tags attached. Joanne needed an organization to underwrite the operational expenses of her newly conceived tournament. She went to the local newspaper. "Not enough interest in golf," harrumphed the sports editor in an abysmal demonstration of deficient sports knowledge.

So Joanne approached one of her "snowbird" students. ("Snowbirds" are persons from the northern states who migrate to Arizona for the winter.) Lester A. Colman, whose midwestern manufacturing plant made parts for General Motors, asked, "Would a thousand help you out?" Joanne fell off her teaching stool.

"Would it! Oh, wow!"

So the Arizona Silver Belle golf tournament had its beginnings twenty-five years ago.

The Silver Belle was originally a homespun event featuring picnics by the Verde River. Six-year-olds were invited to play. Joanne's brother John, a talented commercial artist, designed trophies fashioned after Southwestern Native American art.

Through its twenty-five-year history, the Arizona Silver Belle has attracted 2,000 entrants. Many of these players were adequately skilled to graduate onto the LPGA tour—Beth Daniel, Danielle and Dana Ammacapane, Lauren Howe, Jennie Lidback, Lauri Mertens, Mary Bea Porter-King, Jody Rosenthal-Anshutz, Brandie Burton, Heather and Missie Farr, Nancy Harvey, Chris Johnson, Alice Miller, Tina Tombs-Purtzer, Vicki Singleton, and Robin Walton.

But the price of running the Silver Belle escalated until it reached $12,000 in the late 1980s. Printing costs, greens fees, advertising, the

price of the Kachina dolls later given as prizes—all added up to a budget the sponsoring committee, not experienced at fund raising, could not visualize meeting.

Then one day early in 1990, Joanne described the Silver Belle to Patty. It was an event for young women trapped in the limbo between junior golf and adult tournaments, a competition for fourteen- to twenty-four-year-olds. Patty said that yes, she'd sponsor the Silver Belle. The Patty Sheehan Silver Belle. Patty did not suggest the retitling of the tournament; Joanne proposed the name modification in honor of the tournament's savior.

The tournament itself was in progress at the Karsten Golf Course at Arizona State University when the telephone call from Reno came in. "I was like a midget race car driver in that golf cart," Joanne recalled," tearing out on the course to tell all of our committee members that the Silver Belle had been saved, that Patty Sheehan—yes, *the Patty Sheehan*— had saved the Silver Belle."

Patty appeared in person at the first Silver Belle under her sponsorship. Joanne Winter was flabbergasted at Patty's speech at the banquet. "*She* thanked *us*," recalled an incredulous Joanne, "for allowing her to participate in the tourna-

THE SHEEHAN FAMILY CLASSIC

Everybody who knows which end of the golf club to hold and who lives within a generous radius of Middlebury, Vermont, enters the Sheehan Family Classic, an ongoing summer tournament instigated by the dedicated Sheehan humanitarian, Patty. The Classic proudly presented this breakdown of revenues and recipients.

The net revenues for the tournaments from 1991 through 1995 were $60,000, distributed as follows:

Memorial Sports Center	$27,500
Hook a Kid on Golf Program	6,000
High School Golf Team	500
Middlebury Ski Club	4,500
Porter Hospital Campaign	3,700
Vermont Interactive Television	3,000
Boy and Girl Scouts	1,800
High School Scholarships	4,000
Elderly Services	3,000
American Cancer Society	4,000
Addison County Vo-Tech Adult	1,000
Rotary Foundation	1,000
TOTAL	**$60,000**

ment. Can you imagine that? *We* allowed her to participate. But that's Patty."

Patty paid all of the tournament expenses for five years, after which she recommended that the Silver Belle committee seek out more local backing—perhaps even the local newspaper!

By then 400 talented young women had been awarded the opportunity to play competitive golf, a gift from Patty Sheehan whose generosity is a matter of everyday giving.

After the earthquake of October 17, 1989, 5,000 feet of 16 mm movies from tour days in the forties, fifties, and sixties lay in rubble in this author's northern California home. The film, including footage of the original Hall of Famers (Zaharias, Berg, Suggs, and Jameson) and the swings of all of the competitors in our early days, needed to be put on videotape and preserved in the archives at LPGA headquarters. But it would take time and money to do that.

Patty Sheehan said, "How much?" About $300.

Patty reached for her checkbook and wrote out a check for $300.

Ruth and Ed Jones had a 4^1/2-year-old shih-tzu, Milty, who was developing cataracts, the result of early-onset diabetes. His vision was deteriorating rapidly. With no pet health insurance (offered in California, but not Nevada), the Joneses decided they would have surgery on only one of Milty's eyes, at a price of $900.

They mentioned their decision to Patty and Rebecca Gaston. "The next thing we knew," related Ed, "Patty and Becky gave us a check for $900."

"We want to be sure," explained Rebecca, "that Milty can see *both* his girl friends, Sherlock and Quincey."

"I don't have just one major charity right now," Patty said in late September 1995. She had just come from the golf course where her

Patty Sheehan Celebrity Classic was being played. Celebrity Classic was a fund raiser for the Girls and Boys Clubs of Truckee Meadows.

The Community Center of Middlebury, Vermont, sponsors sports activities for youths. The Sheehan Family Classic, which raises money for a variety of local organizations, is its centerpiece event. "*Everybody plays,*" exults Patty.

A refreshing contrast from the greed-driven athletes of today who charge significant sums just for autographs, Patty donates all her time for these events. Of course, greed is not limited to modern times. Babe Zaharias, who was resoundingly lauded for her efforts on behalf of the Damon Runyon Cancer Fund, left a folder of letters from Damon Runyan in the LPGA's miniscule files when she resigned after a two-month term as LPGA Tournament Director. All the letters guaranteed Babe $1,200 per "charity" appearance. In 1953 $1,200 was a substantial gratuity for a half day's work.

"Hey, if you're doing it for a charity," protests Patty Sheehan, "you do it for *free.*"

Patty pulled her golf glove off following a day-long photo shoot. A member of the photo crew offered her the envelope for storing the glove. "Nope, this glove doesn't go back in its envelope," laughed

Patty. "I just autograph it and send if off to Mom in Vermont. She turns around and sells them for ten dollars each and then gives the money to charity."

"I've made $1,400 so far," reported the one-woman fundraiser, Leslie Sheehan. "The money goes to the Middlebury Memorial Sports Center."

From the mundane to the glorious, from tearjerkers to cheers, Patty lets the money pour from her generous heart. Whether it's an ice skating rink in Middlebury or a home for abused girls in Santa Cruz or the gift of sight for a special dog, Patty Sheehan knows how to make a difference in lives.

READING GREENS

Images of me lining up a putt are so distinctive that they have wound up on champagne bottle labels. Distinctive? Yeah. I have this unusual habit of cupping my left hand over the tip of my visor. You'd like to think, wouldn't you, that therein lies the secret to putting success? Well, it doesn't. I started using this posture when, as an amateur, I saw a caddie cupping his left hand over his visor.

Many average players attempt to copy a mannerism of a particular player in hopes it will provide a mystical advantage. Hitch up your pants like Arnold Palmer does before a shot, and you'll hit it better. Right? Wrong. Very wrong.

I've watched the women play on ladies day, or the ladies play on women's day, whichever. Almost nobody lines up putts correctly. And almost nobody three-putts because she is six or eight feet off line on her approach putt. She three-putts because she is six feet long or eight feet short. She failed to read the green, or if she did attempt to read it, she read it wrong.

Here are some brief hints on lining up putts so that you keep all of the ladies on women's day happy about your pace of play and avoid illiteracy on the putting green:

1. **Be aware of the entire slope on which the golf course is built.** We hear phrases like "the greens will break away from the mountains" or "the greens break

READING GREENS
continued

toward the ocean." This does *not* mean that every putt will break away from the mountains or that every putt will break toward the ocean. The generalization simply means that the putt will break *more* away from the mountains or toward the ocean than you see it will when looking at only your line of putt.

2. **Be aware of the entire slope of the individual green.** I never wait until I'm on the green to start lining up a putt. I am looking at the green as I approach it. Is the left side of the green higher than the right side, or vice versa? Is the back of the green much higher than the front of the green? Rarely will the front of the green be significantly higher than the back.

3. **Feel the green with your feet as you walk onto it.** Crusty, crunchy? It's going to be fast. Long and unmown (typical on ladies day) and soft underfoot? It's going to be slow.

4. **Try to position yourself so you can align your putt while someone else is putting.** You will want to stay out of her line of vision, of course.

5. **Know that your first impression of your putt is probably the correct one.** Rarely is it necessary for you to go to the opposite side of your putt for another look. Actually, more can be learned about a putt by looking at it from the side—at right angles to the line—as far as the uphill/downhill question is concerned.

I have a distinctive way of lining up putts. I developed this mannerism of cupping my left hand over the bill of my visor after watching a caddy do this in my amateur days. Should you copy this in hopes of improving your ability to read a green? No way!
© Rick Sharp

READING GREENS
continued

6. The grain—the direction the grass is growing—probably
   should not be factored in by higher-handicap players,
   especially those playing on bent grass greens that are verticut. Now, bermuda and Tiffin (a type of bermuda which
   has been to the USGA's "college") are different matters.
   That magnificent putter from South Africa, Bobby Locke,
   had a method of reading grain that was quick and effective. A short time after the greens have been mowed, the
   grass on one side of the cup will turn brown while that on
   the other side will remain green. **The grain will run
   across the hole toward the brown side.** This may
   make the putt faster, slower, or the break more to the right
   or to the left.

What causes the brown side? Picture the hole cutter, that $4^1/4$-inch metal sleeve, cutting into the green. On the side of the cup from which the grain is coming, the blades of grass will be lying flat so only the blades will be cut. On the opposite side of the cup, the blades will be growing away from the cup, and the roots will be exposed. When the roots are cut the blades die and turn brown.

"Which way is west?" Ben Hogan once asked his befuddled cad-die. Now, I don't recommend you carry a magnetic compass with you on the course. One PGA professional whose name escapes me did just that and drew a reprimand from the rules purists. "Artificial aid," it's called.

"Which way is west?" may not be overkill for a golfer of Ben Hogan's skill level, but it might be for a 36-handicapper. Why does west matter? Because grass, like other growing plants, is *phototropic*, which means it turns toward the source of light, or the sun. For you "Which way is west?" is probably comparable to Bob Hope asking what time the greens were mowed. It is simply information you will probably not be able to use effectively.

ED AND I CHAT ABOUT TOUGH PUTTS

"Why is it," I asked Ed in one of our innumerable gabfests about golf, "that left-to-right breaking putts are more difficult than right-to-left breaks?"

Ed answered, "I always felt like the ball was going away from me. I always wound up right of where I wanted to go. On a right-to-left break I felt I was putting the ball into myself. There's no doubt that right-to-lefts are much easier to putt than left-to-rights."

I've heard that Walter Hagen recommended this simple technique on left-to-right breaking putts: open up your stance a bit. Then just putt to the point where you think the putt will break. Two inch break to the right? Aim two inches left of the cup and disregard the cup.

"Do you like hitting the ball on the toe when you have an impossibly fast downhill putt?" I asked.

The theory of hitting the ball on the toe of the putter is that you are not hitting the ball on the "sweet spot" of the putter; you are not putting the concentration of weight into the ball. It's the same idea as when you hit a ball with other than the sweet spot of an iron or wood; the ball is not going to go as far.

Ed said, "That was a distraction to me. I got so involved with hitting it on the toe I forgot how hard I was going to hit it. But don't listen to me. I'm not the world's best downhill putter."

Some people swear by the effectiveness of hitting the ball on the toe on slippery downhill putts. Try a few putts hit on the toe and you'll see the result. You may not be like Eddie and get distracted so easily. For you, hitting the ball on the toe just might work. It does for me!

CHAPTER SEVEN

A CARICATURE
OF LIVING

The problems and harassments of living and working are magnified by the traveling life of the tour. Doing the laundry is an example. At home, one stuffs the soiled clothes in a basket, walks down the hall to the laundry room, pulls a box of detergent from a shelf, loads up the machine, and walks off to other chores or pleasures while the machine does its task. On tour one must hunt down a laundromat (the one used last year has inevitably closed), buy some detergent, load the machine, and sit reading a paperback for an hour or two. The laundry chore probably still tops the list as most hated on the LPGA tour.

Neither is the weekly packing and unpacking among treasured pastimes. Airports are not preferred haunts. Galleries full of unfamiliar faces are tension-producing despite the rush the players get from the applause. Galleryites can be abysmally insensitive about comments they make. So can pro-am partners. "I am not your horse,"

retorted Patty Sheehan to one partner, who had just called her that.

Then there is an additional intrusion on what players would like to perceive as their privacy.

The media sniffs around the periphery of the LPGA tour in pursuit of the scent of controversy. Too often the quest is rewarded with a Ben Wright story, a cheating scandal, a divorce worthy of front page headlines in the *National Enquirer*, or a star who preferred skiing with her father in Switzerland to defending an LPGA tour title. Patty Sheehan has been in the middle of some of these media-created donnybrooks, never willingly, but always with cautious candor.

"Eddie Jones told me how tough the tour could be," Patty said. "But I don't think the *National Enquirer* had started publishing in Ed's day." Muckraking seems to have increased by the square of the prize money.

The competition itself provided no terrors for Patty. "After all, I've been competing since I was four!

When I first went on tour I had already had twenty years of competition in skiing and in golf."

Tour life has changed dramatically since the LPGA was first organized. For the pioneers in the late forties, travel was only slightly better than covered wagons, as the small troupe caravanned along the two-lane highways that had not yet become interstates, crashing their automobiles with frightening regularity.

Their journey was not in 500-mile-an-hour jets that whisk the players to Philadelphia, Miami, Atlanta, Dallas, San Jose, Portland, Seattle, Tokyo, and London. The pioneers hung their golf clothes up in unpretentious motel rooms, often cockroach infested, occasionally equipped with kitchens. Today's leading money winners retreat into residence inns when their day's chores are done, feed their dogs out of hotel china, and only occasionally have to endure the annoyance of lost or late luggage (Patty Sheehan); burglarized vans (Patty Sheehan); muggers who rip expensive rings off fingers, (Jan Stephenson); tournament barbecues that flame amok, charbroiling players instead of hamburgers (Cathy Gerring); or randomly fired bullets through necks of players making innocent visits to a convenience store (Kim Williams).

When one adds up the airway miles, it's little wonder the touring poodles, Sherlock and Quincey, are deliriously happy to trot out of their travel crates and romp.

Rebecca Gaston, Patty's manager, tried to get them frequent flyer accounts, but American Airlines wouldn't go for the idea. So imaginative and resourceful Becky marched into the offices of Reno Air and negotiated what Patty thinks is an LPGA first, an individual LPGA tie-in with an airline. "Patty Sheehan" is now written in three-foot-high letters across the nose of one of the airline's MD-80 jets. Patty and Rebecca and Sherlock and Quincey all fly free, whenever their destinations match Reno Air's expanding route structure.

"What do I do when I'm home and off the tour for a week or two or three?" Patty repeats the question put to her. "I dig in my garden. Rearrange the landscaping, putz around in the wine cellar—I have a good collection now. Not many spots left in the cellar. I might even meander over to Hidden Valley, hit a few balls, putt a little, kibbitz with Ed Jones. But I won't do that much. That's what weeks off are about—getting away from golf."

An artificial turf installer, Mark Matheny of Santa Rosa, California, offered to build a putting green in Patty's backyard. Patty declined with thanks. "Don't want anything around to remind me of golf." A few household items seem to contradict her declaration. On her mantel (in 1994), the National Open trophy reposed along with a smaller replica that Rebecca had created after Patty's 1992 win. On the end table by Patty's favorite recliner was the two-foot-high bronze statue of Patty in follow-through position, presented to her from Rebecca at the Hall of Fame banquet. Nothing around to remind you of golf?

Patty grinned, trapped in the farcical nature of her own declaration, "Well, nothing around that reminds me of practicing."

"Sometimes," said Ed Jones, "Patty will come off the tour and she'll be so pooped she won't feel like hitting any balls. We just sit and talk about her swing problems."

But not too pooped to run with Sherlock and Quincey, or to hoe the weeds out of her corn rows, or to whip up a gourmet low-fat dinner.

Inspired by a French mansion Patty and Rebecca toured on a week-long vacation following a European tournament, Patty Sheehan's fourth home, decorated in French country style, is smilingly called "Chateau la Tour."

Its inception was far from happy. In the early 1980s Patty owned a condominium in Los Gatos, a San Jose suburb, then moved into a 4,000-square-foot showcase in the Santa Cruz Mountains' Scotts Valley. The rustic home sat astride the San Andreas Fault on four acres of redwoods overlooking Monterey Bay. "I should have been suspicious when one of the ceiling beams moved after that five-pointer we had in the spring of '89." The house was ripped off its foundation by the 7.1 disaster of October 17, 1989. "Inside the house looked like fifteen vandals had ransacked it," Patty said.

Rebecca observed perceptively, "The earthquake had destroyed just about all of Patty's earthly possessions. Almost everything she had worked a lifetime building and accumulating. And the house had been so special to her. People don't realize how special homes are for professional athletes who are on the road much of the year. For Patty and other golfers, home is where they go for a vacation. In a matter of fifteen seconds her place of serenity had been destroyed."

After the initial numbing was over, Patty became philosophical. "A lot of people died in the earthquake. Many others were seriously injured. Who knows what might have happened to us had we been home instead of at Candlestick Park, waiting for the World Series to start. We survived, and every day I realize how fortunate I am and how precious life is."

"I had many different feelings after the earthquake. It was unreal when the earthquake hit. You simply cannot believe it is happening. I didn't feel that my home was going to be damaged. Then we kept hearing radio reports about SFO bridges falling and freeway overpasses killing people. We heard nothing from the Santa Cruz area, even though downtown Santa Cruz was a pile of rubble and people had been killed and injured."

Juli and Brian Inkster live in Los Altos, about midway between Candlestick and Patty's house near Santa Cruz. The Inksters' house was thoroughly destroyed. The pool cracked and lost a lot of water. "We saw firsthand what the earthquake could do to a house. Then we realized something could be wrong with my house. The twenty-five-mile drive from Los Altos to Scott's Valley normally required about forty-five minutes; due to rubble and cracks in the roadway we needed three hours to drive the distance on October 18, 1989. Finally we drove up my long uphill driveway. Two plywood cows (made by Bobo) in my vegetable garden were still standing. So everything was kind of cool. But when we opened the front door and walked over the threshold, we noticed a six-inch gap between the threshold and the rest of the house. Then I looked inside. I could not believe what I saw. I was in shock. I wandered around, surveying the damage. We realized we wouldn't be living in the house; it had to be repaired. Grabbing two brooms, Rebecca and I started sweeping up. Everything I owned was broken or damaged. The dust made my allergies flare up." Included in the rubble were the shattered remains of more than 40 of Patty's crystal golf trophies, worth more than $50,000.

Patty continued with the saga of the Loma Prieta Richter scale 7.1 disaster. "As the shock wore off, I would sit down in middle of a room and bawl. The enormity of what had happened just started to hit me. I realized I had a lot of work ahead, that I had no earthquake insurance, that I couldn't live in the house, that I had no place to go." The storage facilities in Santa Cruz were all filled with the belongings of other refugees. Moving vans were all reserved. Literally left out in the cold, Patty Sheehan was homeless. Patty and Rebecca spent the first night after the massive shake sleeping on the front lawn in an early autumn rain. The aftershocks worsened the experience as they lay on the grass, wet, cold and miserable. "We could hear the aftershocks coming, then feel them, then hear them leave. There must have been 100 that night. The sense of insecurity was overwhelming. You think earth is a pretty stable place. When it starts to move and you don't know where the next crack in the ground is going to appear, it makes for a very trying time."

Their young friend Robin Berning, daughter of former LPGA tour star Susie Berning, was then a San Jose State University student and made the tortuous drive from San Jose to Scotts Valley. "Robin gave us a sense of normalcy, a sense of sanity at a time we desperately needed it. Fortunately we had good friends and a large Sheehan family." Patty and Rebecca stayed with good friends and neighbors John and Jill Lewis for a few nights.

After several days of homelessness, of sleeping on the lawn with autumn rains pelting them, their slumbers punctuated by terrifying aftershocks as the ruptured earth settled beneath them, Patty and Rebecca contacted a moving company. "We'd just lie there during the aftershocks, hoping we wouldn't be dumped into Monterey Bay." On October 29, an eighteen wheeler rolled into Scotts Valley and then, with the golf champion's surviving possessions aboard, headed east— for Reno.

Brother Steve was there, with wife Mary. Robert Jr. ("Butch") was there. Ed Jones, Patty's "second father," lived close by with wife

Ruth. Leslie and Bobo phoned from Vermont, where each summer they escaped Palm Springs' inferno. Brother Jack was on the telephone, too, with hang-in-there pep talks. "I feel like I rediscovered my family," said Patty.

Patty soon rented a house in Reno for six months, then spotted a for-sale sign on a 5,000-square-foot, four-bedroom, three-bath home on the sixteenth fairway of Lakeridge Country Club. "Not an attractive feature for us," said Patty. Lakeridge was the only gated community in Reno, but there was no separation between the house and the fairway. Peeping Toms in spiked shoes would walk up the slope from the sixteenth fairway to Patty's living room window and peer in, trying to grab a glimpse of the star. The for-sale sign went up at 2745 Spinnaker in Lakeridge, and Chateau la Tour was conceived in 1993.

Unfortunately, this house had its downside, too. It went way over budget and far past deadline. Bobo Sheehan complained, "Their contractor really put the wood to Patty and Rebecca. Their contractor was a crook." Patty was playing tournaments just to pay for cost overruns. The building project was rubbing frayed nerves raw. Then the house at Lakeridge sold before Chateau was completed. Patty and Rebecca were forced to live with friends

Susan Daw, a nurse, and Dr. Diana Thomas, a Sparks, Nevada pediatrician, until Chateau became habitable seven weeks later, another strain. "We're still good friends," Patty has mentioned.

Going back on the tour was less nerve-wracking than staying in Reno and swearing at sub-contractors. "I learned a new vocabulary," said Patty, "their language."

Even television commentators jumped in to analyze Patty's tournament problems in 1994. "She's building a house," said one. "It happens every time. Build a house and you'll play bad."

As the pain of childbirth may be forgotten at the ecstasy of watching the infant grow through childhood, Patty put behind her the traumas of building Chateau. Life in hotels makes understandable the architectural rarity of this new house; the 6,000-square-foot home has no right angle corners. "We didn't want anything to remind us of hotels," explained manager Rebecca.

It can be disorienting going from level to level, up circular staircases, down dogleg halls, descending into the wine cellar, then heading through doors that lead into unfinished rooms or past the massive natural stone wall that bisects the home.

Chateau la Tour is actually the name of a French wine," explained the owner of Chateau. The country French architecture is very different for this area." Patty derives a lovely feeling of relaxation from finally being in her own place. When Patty and Rebecca finally began unpacking boxes that they had left untouched since the Loma Prieta event, they found belongings they hadn't seen in five or six years. "It was like Christmas," Patty grinned.

"Being home is the only place I find real peace. Y'see, I'm a public person. People know who I am. I have to be on my best behavior 100% of the time. I can't just be myself. At home, I can take off my clothes and run around in the buff if I want to. I can wear grubby clothes.

"I can do things that make me happy, which have absolutely nothing to do with golf. My house is my sanctuary. People ask where I go on vacation. I say, 'I go home.' I have everything I've always wanted right here . . . I didn't have that renting. I am finally at home. I was born and brought up in Vermont where I learned the pleasures of a rural ambiance. Cows, horses, and pastures beat clubhouses and press tents anytime."

As Patty drove up the drive toward Chateau on a spring day in 1995, she said, "I really feel like I'm out of the city here. I'm in the country. The country is peaceful. I love it." Migrating Canada geese honked their agreement overhead.

Patty Sheehan became an emerging star on the LPGA tour at about the same time the infamous Billie Jean King affair erupted onto sports pages and the nation's television screens. The media was in a feeding frenzy. "There are so many obnoxious reporters out there. They ask you the same question sixteen different ways." Rookie Sheehan, with a high naivete index and kid-next-door wholesomeness, was a logical target for reporters' questions. "How do you feel about this?" was a typical inquiry. Said Patty, "Right after the Billie Jean King thing there was a lot of harassment of the players by reporters. *National Enquirer* offered some big bucks to some of the younger players to reveal who were the lesbians on the tour."

Fortunately, impoverished though they may have been, none of the rookies relinquished what would have been an interesting list.

Patty sputtered in indignation, "Those reporters wouldn't have talked to me for very long! They don't like to hear you being noncommital. They want you to say something, to speak out about it. I'm not into that; I'm not into speaking out about controversial

issues." Then Patty grinned her famous Colgate-buffed grin. "It's just fun to tell them things they don't want to hear."

Such as? "Have I had any bad experiences with lesbians on the tour? No, I haven't had any bad experiences. And I haven't observed anyone else having bad experiences."

Then reporters would get to their real point. How did Patty feel about gays on the tour?

Patty snapped back, "Well, I don't care. They don't bother me; I don't bother them. It's like Ray Volpe, our commissioner, said, 'You're going to find gays in any organization.'"

Look and you'll find lesbians in the American Medical Association, the American Dental Association, the American Bar Association, on your alma mater's faculty, as Girl Scout and Campfire Girl leaders, as flight attendants, as tennis professionals, as real estate salespersons. Why does the LPGA quake in its spikes every time the lesbian issue grabs headlines? Why have the LPGA officials and players hit their denial mode button in panic on several occasions in the past twenty-five years?

The LPGA suffers from a massive case of homophobia—far exceeding that of corporate America.

Wrote San Francisco newspaper

columnist Jon Carroll, "I hope one day to live in a world in which the LPGA commissioner can say: 'Our lesbian golfers, and there are many of them, serve as a shining example for young women across the nation, and any implication that they are injuring the sport is not true.

"But the LPGA has a long history of promoting the Closet as the proper residence for Sapphic Americans. It produces reams of publicity about the supportive husbands of the married golfers, about the cute kids of the motherly golfers, and not one word about the longtime companions of the gay golfers."

Joan Ryan, also writing in the *San Francisco Chronicle*, observed, "For all of the uproar about Ben Wright's remarks, they weren't as disturbing as the response to them....We are so afraid of confronting our own cultural biases, of revealing ourselves to be even a little bit sexist, racist, or homophobic, that we say nothing. We don't want to offend....And I wish the LPGA would have seized the opportunity to address this very real issue instead of pretending it didn't exist. Acknowledging and then examining biases are the first steps to overcoming them."

"Corporate America," says Heather Wishik of Tufts University, who conducts workshops to help groups shed their crippling homophobia, "is far more tolerant of the gay life style than is the LPGA."

Don Sabo, sports sociologist at D'Youville College in Buffalo, was quoted in an article on the LPGA appearing in *Sports Illustrated.* "The *L* word is very much alive on the LPGA tour, just as it is wherever single women are successful," he observed. "But it's not about sex. It's about power. By calling a woman a lesbian, men can discount a woman's achievements and keep her institutionally subordinate."

The paralyzing fear persists among the athletes that someone in the ranks of women golf professionals may "pull a Martina," and come out.

The most recent LPGA excrement to hit the fan was the widely publicized Ben Wright flap. Ben is a golf commentator for CBS. Every LPGA member was obligated to have an opinion on some level in response to Ben's alleged comments. The commissioner, Charles Meachem, was particularly obligated to make a statement—a long statement.

Meachem said to the assembled media representatives in Wilmington, Delaware, on the Saturday of the LPGA championship, "You can tell obviously that I am angry. The absurdity of this charge both saddens and angers me. I am sad because it is an unfair attack—a cheap shot—on a group of talented professional women that I truly love and genuinely respect.

"Frankly, after four and one half years in this job I find that I am increasingly annoyed and impatient with those kinds of comments—for several reasons." Meachem then pointed out the LPGA's growth. Prize money was up 40 percent; eighteen sponsors had increased prize money. These facts resoundingly contradict the assertion that the *L* in LPGA stands for lesbian and that the organization has an image problem.

Dr. Pat Griffin, associate professor of Social Justice Education at the University of Massachusetts, said "Heterosexual, bisexual, lesbian—what does it matter, as long as they play good golf?" Dr. Griffin specializes in homophobia workshops for corporations and institutions. She also said, "I was disappointed in the response of the LPGA commissioner and of the players to the Ben Wright controversy. Denying does not make the problem [of the recurring accusations] disappear."

Ben Wright had joined a distinguished group, which includes PGA tourist Tom Watson, in charging that lesbianism hurts the LPGA with sponsors. The distinction is that Tom was quoted in the emi-

nent journal, *Golf World*, and did not refute his statements. Ben was quoted by a reporter, Valerie Helmbreck of the *Wilmington News Journal*, preceding the 1995 LPGA Championship there. Ben denied that he made the comments, and Helmbreck did not tape the interview. She claims, however, that she takes accurate notes.

Ben Wright was called to CBS headquarters in New York to explain to officials. Watson was never invited to the carpet by the PGA. Helmbreck quoted Wright as saying, "When it gets to the corporate level, that's [lesbianism] not going to fly. They're going to a butch game and that furthers the bad image of the game."

Nancy Lopez responded, "I wonder why it is that men can room together and women can't? I don't even feel comfortable having a woman roommate on the tour anymore. Why doesn't he talk about men on the tour who fool around on their wives?"

Nancy Lopez should know the answer to that last question. The advent of the 1990s has not rid society of its treasured double standard.

Amy Alcott said, "People out here watching the tournament don't care about what anyone else does in their bedroom."

Lauri Merten called Wright a

"jerk" and insisted he be fired.

Patty Sheehan said, "I think it's because we're women athletes that we don't get much TV coverage." Asked if some corporate sponsors refused to support lesbian golfers, Patty answered, "I can only speak for myself, and I have never come across that problem in dealing with sponsors."

Patty added privately, "Lesbianism isn't the problem. Homophobia is."

Ben Wright might be startled to know that some of the most beautiful, feminine players on the LPGA tour are lesbians.

Wright also observed that women golfers are "handicapped in having boobs. It's not easy for them to keep the left arm straight and that's one of the tenets of the game. Their boobs get in the way." He lamely claimed JoAnne Carner was first to make that observation, and he merely picked up the quote from her.

A quick leafing through any golf publication will reveal a rebuttal to Wright's anatomical analysis. Many of the leading male professionals do not maintain an extended left arm at the top of the backswing. Fred Couples, Nick Price, Lee Trevino, Curtis Strange, and Bernhard Langher, all boobless, are leading examples. Boobs in the way? Is the straight left arm even one of the tenets of the game? Wright relinquished his credi-

bility with that statement.

In 1987 Patty found herself mired in a very different controversy when her father issued a mind-numbing invitation to his youngest child. "I've been invited to an Olympic reunion in Switzerland. It's a get-together with people who have been important in my life. Could you go with me to represent the family? Incidentally, we'd get to do a little skiing."

The date of the European trip conflicted with the Sarasota Open, which Patty had won the previous two years. Traditionally, defending champions defend their titles. Patty, after agonizing for days, decided to go with Bobo, and so informed Sarasota tournament officials.

Jim Achenbach, writing for the Sarasota newspaper, failed to understand the importance of Bobo Sheehan in Patty's life, or skiing, or the Olympics, site of Patty's conception. Achenbach wrote a critical column.

Patty called the reporter, then in Anaheim, California, to cover the Super Bowl. "I'm holding your column," she said, her voice crammed with emotion. "It kind of hurts my feelings. For people to come down on me, it's distressing.

"It was a hard decision to make," Patty continued. "I weighed both sides of it. It took me a long time to figure out what I should do."

Sarasota golf fans were first led

to believe that Patty had simply opted to go skiing the week of the Sarasota Classic. "Some folks won't understand," she admitted. "But I only have one father. It's difficult for me to turn my back on somebody so important in my life. The main reason is that I love my father and I'm doing this for him. It's an Olympic occasion."

She explained to Achenbach the importance to her of the Sarasota Classic. "I'm definitely going to miss this," she said. Achenbach wasn't buying.

"While she skis?" he asked.

Maybe it's tough for people from Florida to understand the lure of a winter sport. But Patty thought Achenbach might understand her relationship with her father, and Bobo Sheehan's relationship to the Olympic Games.

The LPGA didn't buy it either. The association smacked Patty with a fine for "conduct unbecoming a professional golfer." (Loyalty to one's parents is "conduct unbecoming"?) Patty easily paid the tariff with her winnings from the Sarasota Classic in 1988. At the prize presentation, she said she would return. "All of you can quit bugging me about ski gloves, hats, and all that other stuff. I am here to stay. "

The tour is not all drudgery. In 1982 Vivian Brownlee and Mary Dwyer formed the Unplayable Lies, the unofficial LPGA band. Patty Sheehan was amazed at how many musicians could be recruited from LPGA ranks. Mary Dwyer, an accomplished pianist, was also the band's writer, arranger, and conductor. Patty Sheehan was one of the band's singers, in quartet with Lauren Howe, Judy Dickinson, and Lynn Adams. Vivian Brownlee played the mandolin, Julie Stanger Pyne the banjo. Beverly Klass, Donna White, Melissa Whitmore, and Cathy Morse were on four guitars. Robin Walton blew the trumpet. Barbara Moxness fiddled. Kathy Postlewait and Jerilyn Britz played the accordion, Dot Germain the triangle. Martha Nause, Debbie Raso, Muffin Spencer-Devlin, Debbie Austin, Janet Anderson, Marlene Hagge, and Linda Hunt were frequent participants. The chorus line consisted of Jan Stephenson, Myra Van House (now Blackwelder), and Dale Eggeling.

The Unplayable Lies was decades removed from the two-woman LPGA show of the fifties, with Babe Zaharias on the harmonica and Betty Dodd on the guitar, singing "My Little Mama Came A-Knockin,'" "The Weathervane Song," "Detour," and "I Felt a Little Teardrop Start."

Clad in white blouses, blue pants, red bow ties, and straw hats, the ten-person Unplayable Lies group specialized in American classics: "Yankee Doodle Dandy," "Bill Bailey," "Grand Old Flag."

Group leader Mary Dwyer commented, "Patty's got a good voice. And she really enjoys it. I think it allows her a chance to let down her hair. When Patty can't make a performance, we really miss her. Every time she sang with us, she won," Dwyer added. In 1983 that meant singing quartets and a quartet of wins.

The Unplayable Lies entertained at pro-am parties and special celebratory events such as the thirtieth anniversary of the Women's National Open in Salem, Massassachutts, in 1984.

Any revelers who enjoyed the group at festivities would agree they were good and they were entertaining. The tour's personnel turnover, however, doomed the group, particularly when Mary Dwyer retired to a Palm Springs teaching tee in the late 1980s. "We kinda fell apart," Patty Sheehan lamented.

Despite her participation in the Unplayable Lies, Patty is persistent in saying she does not affiliate with any of the many cliques extant on the tour. Never has, never will. There's the Bible study group, the tour's Christian Coalition. There are the marrieds, the young mothers, the fishing fanatics. There are the LeRoy Nieman art collectors. Name your interest and there's probably a group in the LPGA either formally or loosely organized around that interest.

"I really don't have a *best friend* on tour," Patty said in 1981. Since 1987 her manager and best friend Rebecca Gaston has filled that void.

"I hate the travelling part of the tour!" Patty emphasizes. Rebecca now eases that strain for her—making airline and hotel reservations, taking Sherlock and Quincey to the veterinarian for their health certificates, organizing the luggage. Except for the addition of canine travelling companions, Patty had to do it herself when she first joined the tour. "I didn't have Mom and Dad to take care of me. That'll mature you fast!"

Patty observes, "Off tour, people are always asking me about this player or that player. 'How is she to play with?' 'Is she as much of a sour puss as she looks on TV?' 'She looks like fun. Is she?' I get all kinds of questions."

"Beth Daniel is probably the best player of our age group, the thirty-five to forty gang. That includes Betsy King, Nancy Lopez, Amy Alcott, and myself." But Patty points out that Beth has been injury plagued, or "she would have forty wins by now." Patty credits Beth with a wonderful game, a fiery disposition. "Daniel loves competition. She owns a beautiful golf swing and she's comfortable on the course. I've always admired Beth, but she has had to learn to deal with the media. " The media has not always represented Beth's explosiveness fairly, according to Patty. Beth's resentment shows in her occasional coolness toward the media. "She has done a lot for the game, giving clinics, working with juniors. Beth knows there is more in life than golf and that's more than you can say about most of the players. She loves to fish. And Beth Daniel is a loyal friend."

On mention of some of her competitors' names, Patty responds by rolling her eyes or by emitting a large sigh. "Betsy King is a complicated person. I like her. She is very bright, very passionate about golf and about her golf swing. She is a great gutsy fighter of a competitor." Patty emphasizes Betsy's religious fervor. "She holds specific beliefs and does not vary." For that reason many of her peers and galleryites misunderstand her; they think she does not have a fun side. According to Patty, she does, even though she finds it difficult releasing herself to have fun.

Meg Mallon? "A good friend. A delight to play with. Meg has a fine golf swing, an even temperament." Patty is delighted that Meg could share in all of the festivities and pranks of her Hall of Fame induc-

tion in November 1993.

The name Amy Alcott elicits no eye rolling or colossal sighs from Patty. Instead, Patty smiles. "What a great spirit for the game, even without being wrapped up in it!" Alcott has Los Angeles-Pacific Palisades-Hollywood origins, providing this eminent story and joke teller with a unique perspective on life. "Gosh!" exclaims Patty. "She's been on the tour since she was eighteen—and she's thirty-nine now. According to my arithmetic that's twenty-one years! I personally think Amy will win again and make the LPGA Hall of Fame. Amy will win when she wants to win.

"Now, Dawn Coe-Jones is a late bloomer. She really didn't start to come into the game until she got married." Patty confesses to not know Dawn all that well, but recognizes her as charismatic; Dawn has a good time on the golf course. "Canadians seem to have a different outlook on golf and life; they live life more fully. I see them having a ball, kidding, playing around."

Nancy Lopez is a woman of changed motivations. She loves being around Ray (her husband, Ray Knight, former major-league baseball star, one-time World Series MVP, now retired) and the kids, of which there are three. Patty says of Nancy, "She's gracious, but a great competitor. She never gives up." Patty admires Nancy's marvelous rapport with people, admires how she can coax effective shot-making out of a unique, homegrown swing style.

Ah, Dottie Mochrie. "Talk about intense! Dottie has been one of the best players of the last five or six years. She's fiery and emotional." But Patty points out that Dottie still concentrates well. "Look at her after she has hit a shot; you know how she has hit it. You know, moment to moment, exactly how she feels."

Does Patty have an opinion on the Mochrie-originated procedure of having the caddie check her alignment on every shot through the green, a technique now being copied by a number of the LPGA professionals. "Yeah, I have an opinion. I don't like it. I figure if you can't line yourself up, you probably shouldn't be out here. I think it looks bush league. Several years ago the USGA ruled against having your caddie stand on your line before and during your entire putt, like Johnny Miller did. I think they should rule against your caddie aligning you for full shots, too."

Who's the best of the younger set, the under twenty-fives? Patty responds quickly, "Oh, Brandie Burton, of course. She's even-keeled, controlled. She has a wonderful sense about her. She's a smart player—and very strong and very

mature." While Patty is an advocate of young golfers staying in school, she thinks Brandie, who walked off the Arizona State campus at the end of her freshman year and onto the tour, was mature enough to know what was right for her. Brandie is unusual, Patty observes, because she didn't come out cocky and think she'd take over the golf world. She came on tour, mature beyond her years. Her only defect, as Patty sees it, is not making good decisions about dealing with injuries, of which she has had many. Brandie has apparently bought the philosophy that there's something heroic about playing with pain; she keeps on playing in spite of her bad wrists. "That doesn't help the injury," says Sheehan, who assuredly knows about such matters. "Brandie Burton loves to play every day of her life."

Vicki Goetz? Those glacial blue eyes roll again. "She came on the tour under tremendous pressure because of her great amateur record and her tremendous short game. But Vicki is not strong enough physically. And those big expectations for her hurt her."

About Pat Bradley? "What a great competitor!" Like Sheehan, Bradley was inspired by her golfing family. "Pat does not get involved in conversations on the course," Patty observed. "Nor off the course either, for that matter. She doesn't socialize much; she keeps to herself and just gets her job done."

JoAnne Carner is great fun, according to Patty—she always goes full tilt and is fun to compete against. "It's amazing she can keep motivated at her age [now fifty-six]."

The winningest professional of all, Kathy Whitworth, is one with whom Patty especially enjoys playing. "Toward the end of her playing career, Kathy struggled quite a bit. She has always been supportive of me and had nothing but nice things to say to me." Patty sees Kathy as a great player with enormous talent, but who has trouble conveying those facts to others.

"Now there is an extremely talented player, that Laura Davies," says Patty. "She is extraordinarily strong." Why doesn't Davies win every tournament, as far as she hits the ball? Patty answers, "Because she's not always focused, concentrating." Laura digresses to other sports because she loves them, especially soccer. "She's easy to play with," adds Patty. "It's entertaining to watch her." Davies enjoys competition. Her self-taught, slashing, off-the-feet swing is not classic. "She gets away with it," says Patty, "because she is so strong."

Patty brightens at the mention of Ayoko Okamoto. "One of my favorite people to play with."

Okamoto is a spirited superstar, Patty observes, who is often uncomfortable because Japanese journalists permit her so little privacy. An army of Japanese, armed with gargantuan telephoto cameras, follow her at every tournament. "Ayoko was fun to get to know," Patty remembers, "because when she first came here to play she spoke no English. A lot of us tried to teach her a few English words every day, some of them good words, some of them bad words." Patty points out Ayoko's most admirable qualities: a wonderful swing tempo, very controlled, easy to play with, a great sense of humor.

Does life endure after a player enters the LPGA Hall of Fame? How does Patty Sheehan visualize her life after the tour ceases to be fun for her? Can LPGA players, like PGA stars, just slip gracefully from the regular tour to the seniors tour without skipping a beat? Do home and hearth exert a stronger tug on women than on their male counterparts? What are the after-tour career opportunities for LPGA professionals?

"I'm too young just to sit down and be a Hall of Famer." In 1993, when those golden doors of the Hall swung open for her, the thirty-six-year-old Patty outlined her remaining goals for the *San Jose Mercury*'s Dan Hruby: win the

Dinah Shore (she has not yet done so), win another U.S. Open (she has), and win Player-of-the-Year honors for the second time since 1983 (still on hold).

The senior tour? There is no senior tour for women, although there are some occasional tournaments, such as the Sprint, a tagalong event staged with an LPGA regular tour event. Marilynn Smith heroically organized her Founders' Classic, a marvelous event contested for three years in Dallas. But sponsorship has evaporated.

More women's senior events are rumored to be in the works. Former LPGA player Jane Blalock, now in the golf event promotion business, is trying to put together a tour sponsored by Nike. "I visualize about ten tournaments on an LPGA senior tour eventually," predicts Patty Sheehan. Most of the longtime players, Patty Berg, Louise Suggs, Betty Jameson, and others of their era, have gone on to other pursuits because there was no competitive venue for them. Golf teaching or tournament management or college teaching seem to attract them; their clubs get stashed in a neglected corner of the garage.

To attract players, the LPGA has lowered the age for its seniors to forty-five, which means players like Sandra Palmer, who has monopo-lized the few senior events available, can walk off the LPGA tour and into the senior events.

The problems of generating interest in the LPGA seniors are many. LPGA commissioners have in the past shown a strong disinterest in diluting their promotional efforts. The LPGA is competing for sponsors now with the PGA seniors and with the Nike tour; they have no interest in trying to seek out sponsors for tournaments featuring players who have not had previous television exposure. The LPGA's first televised tournament was not until the early 1960s, excluding the original Hall of Famers.

Some of the women themselves—and Big Mama Carner is prominent among them—are reluctant to admit to senior status, or do not want to admit they can no longer compete with the "kids." But despite all these problems, perhaps in seven years, when Patricia Leslie Sheehan turns forty-five, there will be some competitive venue that offers alluring prize money.

Until then, Patty will probably be content at home in Reno, weeding her vegetable garden, throwing sticks for Sherlock and Quincey to chase, pondering where to invest that last $50,000 check from the 1983 bonus. A great deterrent to development of an LPGA senior tour might be women's propensity for hearth and home. Finally off that carborundum tour, the women, whether married with families or not, are content to settle into a stable domesticity. One only has to observe Patty Sheehan by the pool at Chateau la Tour, Sherlock and Quincey on her lap, to realize how little lure the tour has now for her. She is eminently content at home.

Sheehan's current interest for a career is in golf course architecture. She is devouring books on the subject. Except for Alice Dye, wife of the famed architect Pete Dye, there are few women in golf course architecture, none household names. Mary Mills, 1963 Women's National Open champion and holder of a bachelor's degree in philosophy from Millsaps College in Jackson, Mississippi, has returned to college to earn a master's degree in landscape architecture, a foundation for a career in golf course architecture.

Sheehan has assembled an extensive library on the subject. "It's pretty complicated stuff. I'm hoping, once I have a little bit of knowledge and background, some architect will give me a chance to work with him or her. I definitely have ideas on golf courses, different holes, how they should be laid out. So you never know how it might work out until you get a chance."

Patty is currently working with a golf course developer in Angels Camp, California (in the Sierra Nevada foothills near Yosemite National Park), and will represent that club, Greenhorn Creek Country Club, on tour.

"There is much gratification in golf course design. Golf course architects are artists who are both proud of their work and critical of their work. I can't wait for the chance to design a golf course, of knowing I have created something people can enjoy." Patty has served as consultant on golf courses that other people have designed. She has watched architects in action. She has seen their wheels turning. "I can tell they are asking themselves where to put the teeing ground.

"Great course design is like winning a tournament. There is a pride in their accomplishment, of creating golf courses from raw land. Golf architecture is a very technical endeavor. I personally look forward to that challenge."

Patty Sheehan, golf instructor, has a pleasant ring, but that is one shingle that will never be hung in anyone's golf shop. "I'm a 'feel' player," confesses Patty. "I'd be dishonest taking money for trying to analyze someone's golf swing. Although Ed Jones has certainly imbued me with the fundamentals, I would not be good at analyzing someone's swing."

As to a career in meteorology, Patty agrees she has had a lifetime of weather observations. And there is one meteorological principle she can recite with certainty. Rainbows always follow rain delays.

BACKSPIN AND SIDESPIN

There is sure no shortage of misinformation in golf about what makes golf balls rise, what makes them stop, what makes them slice, and what makes them hook. So I think it is appropriate to give you the straight scoop. First, let's define a few golf terms. These, too, are often used incorrectly.

Backspin. A backward spinning motion on the ball. (A factor in the ball rising and stopping on the green.)

Topspin. A forward spinning motion on the ball. (A ball hit with topspin will not rise; flight resulting from club loft will not be maintained.)

Hook. A shot hit by a right-handed golfer that curves to the left.

Pull. A shot hit by a right-handed golfer that flies left without a curve.

Slice. A shot hit by a right-handed golfer that curves to the right.

Push. A shot hit by a right-handed golfer that flies to the right without a curve.

The last four shots listed will be the opposite with a left-handed golfer.

A question golfers frequently ask is, "How can I get more backspin on the ball?"

For starters, keep your clubs clean. Watch me play in a tournament, and you'll see Carl, my caddie, wipe my club off after each shot. That's not just for show; that's control. Keep one end of a golf towel wet and wipe your club after each shot. Those little grooves

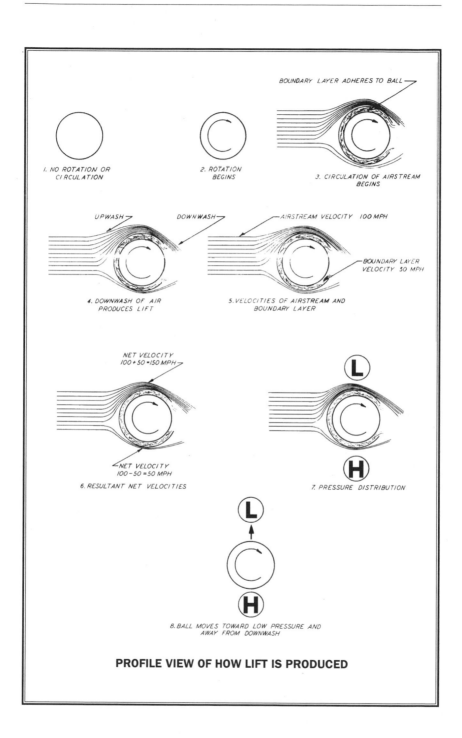

PROFILE VIEW OF HOW LIFT IS PRODUCED

BACKSPIN AND SIDESPIN
continued

in the club are not just decorative, you know. They help give you ball control.

Keep your ball clean, too. The dimples on the ball are aerodynamically designed to produce control. They help the airflow around a ball in flight adhere to the ball so the spinning of the ball will have the most effect. So keep your dimples clean! The ones on the golf ball, I mean.

I think many golfers expect too much in the way of backspin. They see the shots of the professionals spinning backwards after they hit the green and wonder why they can't do the same.

Keep this in mind: there are two factors in making a ball stop on the green. One is trajectory—the angle of ball flight. The other is backspin. Strangely, the shot-club combination that will give the ball the most stop is a full shot with a 5-iron! Why? Because the 5-iron combines the most desirable loft, and thus trajectory, with the

The toe of the club is pointing skyward here. The face of the club is at a right angle to the ground. This position maximizes the club's loft, producing the optimum stop on the ball.
© Cheryl Traendly

Paulette Wrightson, business-woman/golfer, demonstrates keeping her head down too long and the blocking in her swing that results. Blocking means leading with the hands and arms on the downswing so that the natural turning over of the hands at impact (which keeps the clubface square, or at a right angle to the intended line of flight) is "blocked out." Blocking leads to shanked shots, pushes, slices, and topped shots. Although there are other causes of blocking (such as pulling down with the left), keeping your head down too long is a primary contributor. So, keeping your head down only perpetuates the errors you are trying to avoid!

Photo by Betty Hicks

most favorable backspin. But of course, we don't hit a 5-iron when we have ninety yards left to the green. You can't expect a lot of stop on a wedge shot on most of the courses you play. If they kept the greens soft on public courses, for example, they'd be torn up.

So allow for some roll on your approaches—ten to fifteen feet is about right. And be sure you're using the full loft of the club. A high percentage of average golfers hit their approaches with the clubface closed. The ball then goes left and low. And they wonder why the ball doesn't stop.

Check your own backswing, as I'm doing on page 182. At the completion of the backswing, the clubface should be square, not closed. The toe of the club should be pointing skyward, not groundward. Groundward means closed. Closed means left and low.

Many golfers refer glibly to the fact they slice the ball. They don't. They push it. To slice the ball, you have to put a clockwise spin on the ball. True slicers say that doesn't take any talent at all.

BACKSPIN AND SIDESPIN
continued

But slicing the ball actually requires a complex error. You must hit the ball to the right of a line that runs through the ball to the hoped-for target. And you must hit the ball with the clubface open so that the ball spins off the club in a clockwise motion.

This sets up a condition the aerodynamacists call unequal pressure distribution. I won't bore or confuse you with all of the whys of this. Just know that there's lower pressure on the far side of the ball and higher pressure on the near side of the ball. Just like an airplane wing, the ball moves in the direction of lower pressure.

With a hook, the spinning motion is counterclockwise. Again, most women golfers who hit left don't hook it; they pull it. The correction for a pull is quite different than the correction for a hook.

Most women golfers don't slice the ball, either. They push it. They don't hit it hard enough to give the ball any productive clockwise spinning motion.

One of the best corrections I know for a push is to use the Impassifier, the strap around your elbows which will help keep you from blocking on the shot (see page 19).

A common cause of blocking is taking very seriously advice to keep your head down. Keeping your head down is a correction you'll probably overdo. Something's gotta give! Usually you'll give up a good follow-through. Look at the face-on pictures of my full swing (pages 183 and 6) and see how my head rotates shortly after impact with the ball, allowing my right hand to cross over my left. It's the right hand that turns the clubface back into the ball at right angles to the desired line and causes straight shots.

Disregard any advice you hear to leave your right hand out of the shot. Your right hand is very important in your golf swing. *Swing with both hands!* And swing with the Impassifier on. Then give no thought to keeping your head down!

STRAWBERRY LOLLIPOPS: CONCENTRATION

Ed Jones and I were chatting about concentration at Hidden Valley Country Club one day when I was enjoying some days off from the tour.

"What is it?" I asked him. "What is concentration?"

Ed rubbed his chin a moment, as though stimulating thought. "It's the ability to focus the mind totally on one subject and eliminate all of the interruptions and distractions going on around you. It's not an easy thing to learn to do."

"Do you think it can really be learned?" I asked.

"Sure, you learned it. You learned it when you zeroed in on that lollipop at the end of the ski run when you were four."

"A strawberry lollipop," I remembered.

"Well," said Ed, "you've got a lot of strawberry lollipops out on that tour. Because you and Ben Hogan concentrate better than anyone I've seen in golf."

Ed remembered the J and B Putting Tournament in Las Vegas a few years back, which I won despite the roar of the jet airliners taking off from nearby McCarran Airport. "What jets?" was my honest response when someone asked if the noise bothered me. "Typical," said Ed Jones.

I was just so intent and focused on that putting tournament I wouldn't have heard if someone had blown up the Desert Inn where the tournament was being held.

I've just learned to slap down any errant thoughts that intrude on my mind. Kick 'em off the premises and replace them with thoughts only related to the shot at hand. Friends on the tour have confessed to me that instead of thinking of the next shot they have to make, they're composing their acceptance speech when they get the first-place money! You cannot permit that kind of mental wandering.

EARS AND GOLF DON'T MIX

How often I've seen this in the LPGA pro-am tournaments I play in: a male 25-handicapper believes it his solemn obligation to give swing advice to the women golfers in our group. Men, according to our testosterone-revering society, are the font of all sports knowledge. Women rarely, if ever, give unsolicited advice to men.

The trouble with the advice is that it is almost always unrelated to the way the woman is swinging. I can predict, the instant the male opens his mouth, what he will say.

"Take a slow backswing."

"Don't try to kill it."

"Keep your left arm straight."

"Keep your head down."

"You're toe dancing. Keep your left foot flat on the ground."

As I said a few pages earlier, "Keep your head down!" is the worst advice in golf, because keeping your head down locks up your follow-through. If you keep your head down much past impact, you'll "block" on your downswing. That is, you'll have to let your left arm fold up to accommodate that head-down nonsense, and your left arm will block out the natural and desirable turning over of your right hand, as you see in so many of my face-on-view photographs but can't see here. Notice my head is allowed to rotate to follow the swing. That glove in my right back pocket? That's just an extra one I'll be autographing for my mother to sell back in Vermont to benefit a sports center in Middlebury. I hit all my shots, except putts, with a glove on.

© Cheryl Traendly

The advice to keep your left heel on the ground on the backswing should not be given indiscriminately. Shorter golfers tend to let their heels come off the ground more. I sure do. I don't keep my left arm stiff off the top of the backswing, either. No, Ben Wright, it's not because of my boobs, as you are alleged to have said about women golfers. My left arm is comfortably extended at the top of the back swing. Told to keep the left arm straight, women golfers are likely to hyperextend and lock the left arm at the top. My physical therapist friends tell me that such a move can have some direct anatomical consequences, like tennis elbow.

© Cheryl Traendly

And because the woman golfing is receiving advice from an expert, after all, she conscientiously attempts to make the correction(s) and very likely overdoes the correction in the process.

Let's look at this commonly offered advice one by one.

Sure, the backswing is slower than the downswing. The tempo experts tell us the backswing is about one-third of the downswing speed, but don't you *dare* think about that! Swing to waltz music and forget about thinking.

Kill it, but kill it rhythmically. Trying to ease up on a shot can produce other errors. Make that eucalyptus branch sing!

The trouble with women trying to keep the left arm straight is that women can hyperextend their joints and produce unnecessary tension. Let the arc of the swing extend your left arm naturally, rather than thinking about stiffening it.

EARS AND GOLF DON'T MIX
continued

"Keep your head down!" is probably the worst advice in golf. Keeping your head down can be so easily overdone that you sacrifice your follow-through. The result will be deceleration through the ball. *Don't even think about trying to keep your head down.* As your body rotates into the follow-through, your head, being attached to your body, will rotate too—naturally.

Yes, I "toe dance," if you must call it that. In my action shots, my left heel comes off the ground on the backswing of a full swing. It seems to depend upon a player's stature how much he or she lets the left heel come off the ground. Tall, flexible types, such as Mickey Wright, can let the weight roll across their instep and keep their heel fairly close to the turf. Shorter players, as I am at five-foot-three, tend to let the left heel come off more. Just let it happen! If you keep your right knee bent on the backswing and the weight on the inside of the right foot, your left heel won't come too far off the ground. Furthermore, a physical therapist friend says keeping the left heel on the ground is likely to lead to lower back problems. And as golfers, we sure don't want lower back problems. To coax a concluding comment from you on all this, here is a question. Would you let a 25-handicap amateur, even if he is your husband, do your appendectomy? Well, of course not; he isn't a surgeon. Neither is he a golf professional. And he probably does not realize that the golf swing of one champion—even my so-called classic swing—is not going to work for everyone.

CHAPTER EIGHT

THE SCORING TENT

The scoring tent is an area set aside near the eighteenth green where players can retreat and in seclusion double-check their scorecards for accuracy, sign the card they kept throughout the round for another member of their twosome or threesome, and then attest their own card's accuracy.

This chapter is called "The Scoring Tent" because it is a summary of Patty Sheehan's finest memories. The chapter is a montage, covering the Curtis Cup, the British Open, Patty's first major, Nanook of Nevada, Carl the Caddie Machine, and splatter art.

THE CURTIS CUP

In 1980 Patricia Leslie Sheehan was selected by the United States Golf Association to represent the United States in the Curtis Cup matches against a team from the British Isles. Patty had earned the honor on the basis of being runner-up in the 1979 USGA Women's National Amateur Championship. The winner of that tournament, Carolyn Hill, had since become a professional and was thus ineligible.

The Curtis Cup, named in honor of two pioneering golf sisters, Harriot and Margaret Curtis, is an amateur competition, played biennially, alternately in the British Isles and in the United States. The Curtis sisters donated the Paul Revere-designed silver rose cup in 1927, although the team matches were not contested until 1932. Eight players are selected for the U.S. team; the selection process is based upon performances in prior Curtis Cup matches and in USGA and other major women's championships.

"This was my first trip overseas," Patty remembers. "And to represent my country, well, it was pretty awesome." By 1980 Patty was accustomed to wearing uniforms from her San Jose State experience. She simply traded gold and blue for red, white, and blue. The matches were played at St. Pierre Golf and Country Club in Chepstow, Wales.

The United States Team was anchored by a pair of two-time Curtis Cup veterans, Lancy Smith and Carol Semple. Brenda Goldsmith and Judy Oliver had been members of the 1978 squad. The balance of the team, including Patty Sheehan, were team rookies. Mary Hafeman was Women's Western Amateur Champion. Terri Moody had been low amateur in the 1979 Women's Open. Lori Castillo was reigning USGA Women's Amateur Public Links Champion. Lori had also won the 1978 USGA Girls Junior Championship.

Except for Patty Sheehan, none of these players became household names on the LPGA tour. Most did not become professional golfers, for varying valid reasons. There continues to linger in our culture an undercurrent of bias directed at women professionals, as though the world's oldest profession is the only profession in which women should ever participate.

"Hell, why spoil it all?" a home-club member snarled at a national women's amateur champion when she announced she was becoming a professional.

So the cadre of the Curtis Cup team consists of the career ama-teurs. Anne Quast Sander has played in eight Curtis Cup matches, although she missed the 1980 event. Carol Semple Thompson has played in seven. Polly Riley and Barbara McIntyre played a half dozen each.

The format of the matches is both singles competition and four-some competition.

Two matches are played each day over the two-day schedule. Patty Sheehan drew Lori Castillo as her two-ball partner, in which the partners hit alternate shots. They tromped their British-Irish opponents 5 and 3 in the first foursomes match.

Patty and Lori won their four-somes contest the morning of the second day, charging to a three up lead after the first three holes.

Patty won her singles match in the afternoon against Ireland's Mary McKenna, a career Curtis Cupper with experience on five previous teams. Patty played the back nine in one under to win, 3 and 2. "Patty Sheehan . . . is, incidentally," wrote Robert Sommers in the USGA's *Golf Journal*, "a very impressive player." The American team kept its grasp on the Curtis Cup, 13–5, its seventeenth victory in twenty-one matches.

A Nevadan who was conceived in Italy and born in Vermont, who learned most of her golf in Nevada, and who at the time of the cup matches was residing in California, Patricia Leslie Sheehan was the leading point winner for the United States, winning four of four possible. An effort by the Irish players on the British team to claim her as their own failed. The O'Sheehan lineage was not strong enough to stand up to the Stars and Stripes.

SHEEHAN'S FIRST MAJOR

Entry requirements for the LPGA Hall of Fame do not demand a player win a major championship. But if no major is in your record, then to become a Hall member, you must win forty tournaments. The message is clear: win a major. Then you can achieve Hall residence with only thirty-five wins. Better yet, win two majors—separate majors. (Remember, a repeat does not count.)

By the time the LPGA Championship at Jack Nicklaus Golf Center, near Cincinnati, rolled around in 1983, Patty had won five tournaments on the LPGA tour, two of these in the three weeks preceding the LPGA's titular event.

Going into the final round, Sandra Haynie, already winner of two LPGA Championships, a U.S. Women's Open and a Canadian Championship, and inducted into the LPGA Hall of Fame in 1977, led

the 1983 LPGA by four strokes over New Mexican Alexandra Reinhardt. *Golf World* editor Dick Taylor gave a brief history of Sandra Haynie's golf career. Haynie had retired from the tour in 1977, with her wrists and knees scarred from surgery on golf-inflicted injuries, her "psyche burned out," and her stomach in upheaval from the constant pressure of staying "up" for best tournament performances. Haynie came back on tour after a disappointment in a Texas golf-related business venture. Sandra claimed new serenity from lack of pressure to perform for friends, family, and self. "It's easy to explain now how it is. I don't throw up in the morning any more before I tee off."

Sheehan was not considered much of a threat, having just shot a third-round 74, paired with tour buddy Lauren Howe. Patty lurked at seven strokes behind Haynie as they teed off on Sunday. But the prognosticators had failed to reckon on with Patty Sheehan's birdie-binge propensity.

"Well," Patty explains it, "that cup just gets lookin' like a bushel basket." Number ten, birdie. Number eleven, birdie. Number twelve, birdie. Thirteen, birdie. Fourteen, birdie. Five in a row. The five birdies were attached to a front nine 34. Birdies are written on scoreboards in red ink. Patty's score looked like the accounting ledger of a failing business.

Sheehan went into the seventeenth with a two-stroke lead on Haynie. On that hole Sandra threatened by knocking a wedge up within six feet, but gave the hole away, playing the break outside the cup on her putt and missing her birdie try. Sheehan, playing ahead of her rival, had parred, retaining the two-stroke advantage. A two-stroke lead with one hole to play appears to be in the comfort zone, but is not. A two-stroke lead can be vaporized in a split-second spasm of the extensor carpi radialis muscle. Patty parred eighteen, so Sandra needed an eagle to tie. She did not get the eagle. Patty Sheehan became the 1983 LPGA Champion, with a nine-under-par 68–71–74–66 for a 279.

Dick Taylor made some perceptive observations of the LPGA. "A great facet of having a gal like Patty being in the limelight is this: she is fun to watch, and she has fun being watched. None of this isolation-booth golf for her. At Corning when she holed her final birdie in victory she fell over backwards as tension released. The gallery loved her for it." Falling over backwards is one of Patty's least skill-demanding acrobatic performances.

Taylor also bemoaned the fact that Johnny Bench chose to retire, in mid-season and during the LPGA Championship at King's Island. Bench, observed Taylor, wiped the LPGA right off the premier spot on the sports pages. . . . His timing distressed avid local LPGA backers."

If it distressed winner Sheehan, she was quiet about the injustice of the coincidence. Patty has never been, never will be, a limelight grabber. Her clubs speak for her.

In 1984 she became the first player since her idol, Mickey Wright, to win back-to-back LPGA championships. She was sixteen under par in 1984, leaving Beth Daniel and Pat Bradley ten strokes in her wake. Dick Taylor wrote, "Despite all the fresh and cute faces, and great-looking swings, that space between the ears, under head-bones, is the true difference."

That space between Patty Sheehan's ears, under Patty Sheehan's headbones, made the difference at King's Island.

THE BRITISH OPEN

Patty Sheehan's entry into the 1992 Weetabix British Open was a belated one; she became the sixth alternate.

Weetabix? It's a breakfast cereal. No different than saying NabiscoDinahShore as one word. WeetabixBritishOpen. One word.

Sixth alternate became first alternate when four found better ways to spend Open week and dropped out. "I was stuck in the first alternate slot for one month, behind Marta Figuera-Dotti, who was already accepted," Patty recalls. "It got to be a game, my asking Marta every week, 'Well, are you going to play?' and Marta every week responding with a 'Si, si!'"

One week before the tournament Marta withdrew. So the British Open of 1992 was a spur of the moment trip. Patty and her manager, Rebecca Gaston, then in Seattle for the SAFECO Classic, engaged in decision making for an intense two hours. Their conclusion: 1992 might possibly be the only year in which Patty would have a shot at winning both the U.S. and the British Opens in the same year. Another compelling factor was that they were scheduled to go to Scotland only a few days later for the Solheim Cup, the international competition between U.S. women professionals and a women's team representing Europe. They'd go to the British Open.

So now Patty Sheehan had two days rather than a lifetime to prepare. Rebecca was dispatched back to Reno to pack, to make airline reservations, to find a home for Sherlock, the toy poodle who was their only four-legged travelling companion in 1992, and to make all those other arrangements for overseas travel. Sherlock's lodging was simple. "You bet," said Ruth and Ed Jones, "we'll be happy to keep Sherlock."

Patty and Rebecca, despite their frenzied preparations, arrived in London on time. But Patty's golf clubs did not. She played a practice round with borrowed clubs and newly purchased shoes, none of the equipment fitting her at all well. The clubs and shoes finally arrived, two days after their owner.

Familiar clubs in hand and spiked feet back in her own shoes, Patty fired three rounds that added up to eight under par. There were rain delays followed by rainbows. Going into the penultimate round, Patty was leading by one stroke, ahead of a knot of pursuers whose names made it sound like the United Nations was after her: Alfredsson, Neuman, des Campes, de Lorenzi, Dibnah. Throw a Mochrie in there, too.

Patty wore powder blue knickers, a white shirt with blue striping and blue epaulets, and a white visor with Mazda written in blue on it. It was the identical outfit she had worn winning the USGA Open at Oakmont. Superstitious, Patty? "No, I just didn't want to overlook any details that might be important."

By the fourteenth hole of the final round—which is where British television picked up the tournament—Patty had moved to ten under and led Australia's Colleen Dibnah by one stroke. Dibnah and Sheehan combined for the final round pairing.

Dibnah is a powerful woman with a sound swing. She did not appear willing to fold.

Ahead of them, Lisolotte Neuman birdied seventeen to go six under. Patty observed, "Lotte still wasn't much of a threat to me at ten under, after all. But I am the foremost authority on leads in golf. I have made an up-close study of how rapidly they can disappear, and all of the contributing causes of those disappearances.

"I was not relaxed."

"Sometimes I get nervous in a tournament," admits Patty. "I don't throw up in the morning, like Sandra Haynie, but once in a while it's difficult, getting breakfast down." Patty's mouth can feel as dry as Palm Springs after a dehumidifying desert wind has whipped through. Her heart tries to pound its way out of her chest. Breathing can be difficult, even inhaling deeply to induce relaxation. Patty has never been afflicted with the shakes, but she has watched pro-am partners who were shaking so hard she doubted

they'd get the ball teed up. Tension does not ease for golfers after physical activity is initiated, as is the case with more physically active sports. "I've been as nervous on the eighteenth as I have on the first tee."

Dibnah crunched a drive on fifteen, and was hitting a short iron into the green. She parred.

Patty birdied fifteen to treat herself to a two-stroke lead. Her thirst for the kill whetted, Patty drained a 30-footer on sixteen. Her lead was three shots.

"The British male television commentator was, at that moment, saying some mighty complimentary things about my golf swing," recalls Patty. "I'm grateful I couldn't hear them. 'Her club is perfectly parallel at the top of the backswing.' Gad! I can't think about that stuff. I play by feel."

Patricia nailed a drive on seventeen and had only a 110-yard shot left. She hit it three feet from the hole.

Dibnah lipped out on a slightly longer birdie attempt. Lipping out seemed to be contagious. "I did likewise on my three-footer. Damn!" Patty spoke through clenched teeth. "A four-stroke lead would have been more comfortable going into the last hole, if I have the right to use the word *comfortable* in connection with the word *lead*."

Patty was now twelve under going into eighteen. She had to rein herself in. "This is no time to go for broke," said Patty to herself. She fingered her 2-iron, still in the bag. Carl Laib, her caddie, nodded his approval. "I played chicken golf on eighteen," she admitted in the postround interview. "I hit the iron off the tee, hit an iron second to be sure to keep it in the fairway on the par-5 hole, then wedged it up to about ten or twelve feet."

Patty's birdie try was two inches short.

Dibnah stroked her meaningless putt first—she had a lock on second—and holed out, giving Patty Sheehan the courtesy of sinking her tap-in to win the British Open. Prankster Patty hammed it up on that two incher. She addressed the putt and then took a big half swing, as though she were going to hit it with that backswing. The crowd gasped.

"A great win for Sheehan!" was the understatement of the male television commentator.

The Brits have this goose-bump-producing tradition. After the probable winner of their Open has hit the last shot into the eighteenth green, the marshals, who have been holding the crowd back with portable ropes, drop them. "And suddenly there I was on the eigh-teenth fairway of Woburn Golf Club simply inundated by the gallery. That was the neatest part of the whole week there. I could not speak; I was so choked up. Here I was, about to become the first woman ever to win the United States and the British Opens in the same year, jammed in the middle of thousands of golf fans."

That unforgettable moment could not have occurred in a USGA open, of course, which is not meant to denigrate our own national tournament. But the ropes are staked in place for the entire week of a USGA-sponsored national championship. USGA marshals are the "Quiet, please!" people, not rope holders.

For Carl Laib, Patty's caddie, the win was ho hum. The 1992 British was Carl's fourth Open win. He'd won two packing for Betsy King. He was destined to win another.

But the differences between the British Women's Open and the Women's Open Championship of the United States Golf Association do not end at the gallery ropes. Patty has gone in the past and will continue to go to both tournaments with totally different expectations.

The atmospheres of the two tournaments are entirely different. Incredibly, the British Open is much less intense. Is that why the rule makers in the LPGA for several years would not recognize the British Open as a major—or even, in fact, as an official golf tournament? The LPGA has now anointed the British as an LPGA-sanctioned event, though not a major. Perhaps the British is not adequately intense. Patty uses the word "incredibly" because the British are reputed to be stuffy and formal. Not so with their biggest golf tournament.

"On the other hand," Patty continues, "the USGA tournament atmosphere is one of intimidation. The USGA women officials, most of them, have a stern maternal aura about them that once made me feel uncomfortable and probably still does. That doesn't mean I don't love my own mother, because I do. That doesn't mean the USGA people are not very nice ladies, because they are. But when they put on their blue blazers and announce 'Play away, please!' on the first tee, well, I can't help but feel intimidated."

"Intimidated" is a word Patty used frequently in reference to her early years playing USGA tournaments, particularly beginning in 1976, her first Open. Patty explains, "I had early feelings about tournaments in general. It stems from an insecurity of not knowing if I belonged there. For instance, I still don't know all the rules of golf. The rules are terribly complex. There

aren't many golfers who grab a rules book, pull up in front of a fire and 'Curl up their little toes in excitement,' as noted golf observer Herb Graffis once wrote. Only a few people really know all the rules. A lot of USGA people do not know all the rules. Many of the women out there who are rules officials don't know all the rules.

"When I register for a tournament, the intimidation factor immediately kicks in. There's such an enormous amount of material to read and absorb. Fortunately the intimidation factor has eased with age. I try to remember that the officials make mistakes too. They're vulnerable like the rest of us. But if you're a star, people are always watching you. They want to make sure I do things right. They're going to nail me if I do something wrong. They're superior people out there. But these days, what with being in the Hall of Fame, and with two Open wins under my belt, I feel more at ease. I feel I belong there in their golf tournament."

Course setup is another major distinction between the British and U.S. versions of their national championships. The rough is not as difficult in England. "They have those kinds of old fashioned round greens, in contrast to ours," says Patty. In the United States the many shapes of the greens mimic the illustrations of *Gray's Anatomy*, described as they are with names of human anatomical parts, such as kidneys and hearts.

When asked about similarities between the two events (they both are, after all, golf tournaments), the very recognizable Sheehan grin blossoms. "That's easy. There's a very important similarity—those rain delays!"

NANOOK OF NEVADA

In 1985, Patty made her second ski-related decision that inspired the content of sports page columns from San Jose to Sarasota, just as did her decision to go to an Olympic reunion in Switzerland with Bobo, instead of defending her Sarasota Classic title. This time it was her sanity, not her loyalty to the LPGA, that was in question. Reference to the former was jocular, but with an undertone of serious concern. Patty won the Sarasota Classic for the second time in February of 1985 and then announced that the following Friday she would be helicopter skiing in the Ruby Mountains in the northeast corner of Nevada.

Helicopter skiing? "Yeah, they take you in a helicopter to the top of these 11,000-foot-high mountains and drop you and down you go on skis. It's the helicopter ride

that's the most thrilling." Strapping on skis is an activity in which Patty had been engaged since she was eighteen months old.

Wrote *San Jose Mercury News* sports editor Mark Purdy:

"Last weekend Patty Sheehan won a golf tournament and $30,000. This weekend she will put on skis and climb into a helicopter. Then she will be deposited on a Nevada mountain top. Then she will try not to get killed."

"It sounds like a gas to me," Sheehan said Tuesday.

"It sounds like a good way to ruin your backswing. Permanently," countered Purdy.

Sheehan said, "I've led kind of a protected life. It's time to get out and live. What the heck?"

"What the heck? That's perfect. In three words or less, there's no better way to describe Patty Sheehan.

"Sheehan, at 28, is off to the richest start of her golfing career. After the first month of the 1985 LPGA Tour she has won more money than anyone else: $46,650. She should probably be taking a well-deserved week of vacation at her home in Los Gatos. Instead, she's playing Nanook of Nevada."

Purdy interviewed Tammy Alcelay of Ruby Mountain Heli-Ski. "There's always a danger of avalanche," Tammy admitted. "But in eight years we haven't had one accident." Skiers are equipped with automatic beepers so they can be located in an avalanche.

"That's comforting," wrote Purdy. "The one drawback to an avalanche is you can't holler 'fore' and play through. But if it happens, Patty Sheehan will try. Bank on that."

CARL

Carl Laib is a courageous man. He fired his employer, Betsy King.

Betsy had hired the Chicagoan in early 1989. "But how much credit does a caddie deserve for a player's success?" asked one of Patty Sheehan's favorite golf writers, Geoff Russell, in *Golf World*. "Anyone who's spent time with them at tournaments knows *they* aren't even sure. One minute they're bragging about being 'one part coach, one part cheerleader, one part psychologist,' the next they're admitting most good players could win with a baboon pulling their clubs in a little red wagon." There are no baboons on the LPGA tour. There are not even any llamas, those curious beasts being trained at some courses as bag toters. But there is a Carl Laib, the Caddie Machine.

Carl and Betsy won twelve tournaments in three years. The twelve included the U.S. Women's Opens of 1989 and 1990. At the beginning of 1992, however, Betsy King was in warfare with herself. Not satisfied with her performance, she went to a new teaching professional for a makeover. So here was King, battling a new swing when remnants of her old swing were still in place, obstructing. Carl decided their relationship, successful as it had been, had stagnated. He gave Betsy her termination notice.

Betsy wisely returned to her one-time pro, Ed Oldfield, fit the broken pieces back together, and walked off with the LPGA Championship by an eleven-stroke margin.

Patty Sheehan was looking for a new caddie, following a somewhat amicable parting with John Killeen, to whom she had dedicated her win in the 1990 Ping Cellular One in Portland, John's hometown.

The Sheehan-Laib combination didn't initiate its teamwork by incinerating the tour. Patty tied for seventy-seventh in the Sara Lee and failed to make the cut in the Centel. "Once I got the true distance on her shots," Carl explained, "it was easy to learn her game." Patty rewarded him with wins at Rochester and Toledo.

But Patty needed another major (she had two LPGA Championships) to lay a large piece of paving in her road to the Hall of

Fame and to atone for disappointments in the 1990 National Open and at the Dinah Shore (a play-off loss in 1987 in which she missed a three-footer). They got their Open in 1992, and the British—a major in Patty's book, if not in the LPGA's—and another in 1994.

"Carl, do you realize," Geoff Russell asked, "that if you believe U.S. Opens are the most prestigious and pressure-filled events in this country, that makes you the most successful caddie working anywhere in America?"

"I never thought about that," said the cheerful, fun-loving Laib, "but I guess you're right. Who's won more U.S. Opens than I have?"

Carl was born and raised in Chicago. His father had caddied for Virginia Van Wie, USGA national champion in 1932, 1933, and 1934. As a kid Carl caddied at Beverly Country Club, Van Wie's home course, for Gene Littler, Rod Funseth, and Sandra Palmer. When he finally "got a real job," it was as production supervisor for Nabisco and Stroh's Brewing Company. Occasionally, unable to resist the call to the fairways, he'd take a vacation, catch the LPGA tour at some stop, and carry the bag of any professional who was without a toter for the week.

When Carl had his fill of union meetings, of grievances, and of factory work, he left his job for that of a regular tour caddie, working for Nancy Rubin and then for Deb Richard. He soon earned a reputation as the most reliable and prepared bag carrier on the tour. "The Caddie Machine," his peers and the professionals called Laib. He was proud of the label, despite sometimes derogatory overtones.

Geoff Russell wrote of him, "On off weeks, he'll go measure unfamiliar courses. He arrives three hours before most rounds to check pin positions. He charts every shot his player hits during the week.

"Laib will have to take the responsibility of rejuvenation of not one, but two veteran careers."

Russell was referring to the careers of Betsy King and Patty Sheehan.

Following her 1992 triumph at Oakmont, Patty Sheehan did everything but engrave Carl Laib's name onto the National Open trophy. "He took all of the doubt out of every situation we got into," Patty said in gratitude, "because he had gone there early to learn the course and prepare himself." Patty invited Carl into the USGA reception in the Oakmont clubhouse after her victory and offered a toast to his teamwork. "Basically, he works hard even when he isn't getting paid. I think he's the best caddie out here."

Patty flew the Caddie Machine to Woburn and together they added the British Open title to his collection, which after 1994's season, equaled five national championships, only one short of the famous Glenna Collett Vare's string.

Carl's obligations to Patty are complex, but he has volunteered for all of them. "Basically, I try to make it so all Patty has to do is come to the course and play." The Machine has already walked the entire golf course, collecting yardages, locating landing areas, diagramming potential trouble. He maintains a detailed record of her club specifications and assures the specs don't change from week to week. (JoAnne Carner was the victim of a clubhead-bending saboteur a few years ago.) He determines when the club grips are due for a change, which is about every three months. Carl is also vice-president in charge of Patty's nutrition and hydration, two critical physiological considerations that spun out of control in the Atlanta debacle of 1990 and allowed Carl Laib's Betsy King to sneak into the winner's circle. "No, I don't walk the dogs. And no, I don't do the shopping."

"You won't find two future Hall of Famers more different than Patty Sheehan and Betsy King," wrote Geoff Russell. Patty was then one year away from the Hall; Betsy was three years away. Carl Laib, who has spent hours with both, concurs

with Russell. "Betsy is quiet and reserved. Patty is fun-loving and outgoing."

Betsy King hits the ball higher, but driving is a strength they share. "Betsy's forte is in her irons, while Patty's is in her putting. Both of them are excellent in course management. Both of them are easy to get along with, but I had to be careful talking to Betsy. I've never heard her swear. On the other hand, I could say to Patty, 'Hey, you're playing like shit. Let's get going here.'" Carl says he had to motivate King; Sheehan provides her own motivation.

How does Carl feel personally about Patty Sheehan? "She is a very, very good friend, one you trust, rely on. I'm not afraid to ask any question of Patty and Becky."

Carl was proud of the honor he was accorded in October of 1995. Recovering from arthrocropic surgery on his right knee, a condition exacerbated by packing Patty Sheehan's forty-five-pound golf bag for thousands of miles in improper footwear, Carl received an invitation from Stanford University women's golf coach, Tim Baldwin. "They're flying me out there, puttin' me up at the Hyatt and everything," Carl said proudly from his Phoenix home. Visiting university professor, the erudite Carl Laib! Baldwin had observed Laib in action at an LPGA tournament and concluded he could provide what his young charges needed: a lecture on course management and on keeping an accurate yardage book.

Does one have to be a scratch amateur or a Hall of Fame professional to benefit from course management techniques or from keeping a yardage book? Laib doesn't think so. The wisdoms Carl acquired from working with and for course management geniuses Sandra Palmer, Betsy King, and Patty Sheehan are summarized in a sidebar starting on page 63.

One of Patty Sheehan's college teammates, honor student Carol Conidi, at San Jose State University on an academic scholarship, provided a unique twist on course management even as a freshman. "Now what?" asked Carol's coach after Carol had hit a drive into an area of scrawny new trees and off-fairway bare adobe at Almaden Golf and Country Club.

"Well, first," smiled Carol, "you look around for a burrowing animal hole or a staked tree."

Carl Laib would have nodded his approval.

PATTY SHEEHAN, AKA GEORGIA O'KEEFE

Patty Sheehan, artist. Except that Patty Sheehan, artist, did not even own a brush as she completed her most memorable works. Patty's medium is oils. Splatter Art, it is called, a Sheehan copyright. The technique is simple, the results astounding.

"We got the idea one night at Jane Geddes' home when we were trying out new wedges in her garden. We were splattering mud against the side of her garage, and hey, it looked pretty artistic, even though the colors were mud and plaster white.

"So how about," Patty asked, "doing the same thing with oil paints, a golf club, and a canvas?"

The concept hasn't exactly shaken the art world, but Patty has enjoyed some commercial success. "I've sold a few canvases," she smiles. "Every one is different."

Splatter art is accomplished like this: A canvas is mounted vertically on a frame about four feet from the "artist." Artist Patty Sheehan has selected a 3-iron as her brush. "No, I don't know why I chose the 3-iron," laughs Patty.

A large blob of primary color is squeezed onto the mat from which Patty hits. Patty attacks the blob with her classic swing and the head of her 3-iron. Splat! Vivid yellow hits the canvas in an unpredictable pattern of minor and major splats. Then Patty's assistant squeezes a blob of red onto the mat. Swing number two. Red splats blend with yellow and become orange. Some reds and some yellows remain unmixed and produce three colors on the canvas. A generous squeeze of blue now challenges Patty's 3-iron. Splat! Blue-violet blossoms where the blue paint strikes the red. Where blue impacts on yellow, green appears on the canvas.

The painting is marvelous to watch as it emerges. "What is it?" Patty's fans will ask. Patty answsers, "Whatever you want it to be, I guess. Play-off at Oakmont. Double eagle at Rochester. The rough at Indianwood. Rain delay at Atlanta. Just whatever you want it to be."

Patty's artistic creation was pre-served on video tape in Nashville, Tennessee, site of the Sara Lee Classic.

"And how do you feel about the upcoming Sara Lee tournament?" asked her interviewer, after the splattering was over.

Patty grinned, an artist enjoying the therapeutic consequences of her creativity. "Well, I sure feel bet-ter *now*."

WHAT TO DO WHEN THE WHEELS COME OFF

People deal with slumps in different ways. Sometimes taking time off works—two days, one week, two weeks—just to get all of the spookiness out of your mind, then go back and start again. What did I do in 1990 after that Open calamity? Well, I was committed to play the next week, so I played the next week and almost won it. But the Open was really a slump. A *slump* is a prolonged period of playing badly. Two days, two weeks, three weeks, a month, a sea-son—nothing seems to work right.

If you didn't sign a commitment to the LPGA to play next week, hang 'em up for a while. Then you'll go back with a fresh slate.

I'd also suggest you see your teaching professional. It could be you've picked up some little habit that's making you miss enough shots to shatter your confidence. You don't want to "groove" that bad habit, either. Students will go to Ed because they're having trouble, and Ed will say, "So, how long have you been doing this?" When they answer, "Oh, 'bout six months," Ed shudders. By now, the habit is pretty well grooved—and harder to correct.

You keep postponing the lesson because you think the error will cure itself. It won't.

"I know in some cases I've stirred the pot by saying 'try this' or 'try that,'" Ed Jones admits. "By the time you get through trying some things, you've forgotten what you were doing.

Sometimes you just need to get out of the rut."

I remember an LPGA pro asked me once, "Have you ever been in a slump?" I just laughed at her. *Everybody's* been in a slump at one time or another. I missed two cuts in a row once. That's all the slump I'll ever want. When things aren't going well, I just try to get out of my own way. I have a comfort zone. In that comfort zone, I'm not being too critical of myself, too hard on myself.

Something I consider really important is to get away from thoughts on the mechanical parts of the swing. I've seen the following happen to good and intelligent players on the tour. They'll get going badly, or maybe they've been doing rather well and want to do better. They'll say, "I'm going to rebuild from the ground up." They say it as though they're about to indulge in some very courageous act, which will certainly develop their character if not their golf game. Very bad idea!

Or they'll say, "I'm just going to change this move, and then everything will be better." Kathy Whitworth did it. Betsy King did it. The destiny of both was to go back to their original teachers and regain the swings they once had that worked for them.

Books and magazines tend to complicate the swing. They should try to simplify the swing instead. Someone asked the great teacher Harvey Penick at a PGA clinic, "Do you read golf magazines?" He replied, "I read 'em, but I read 'em kinda like I do the funny papers."

I've had some putting problems in the last couple of years. "You went through a phase a few years back," Ed remembers, "when you missed that three-footer to lose a play-off in the Dinah. Eventually you pulled yourself out of it. But the older we get the longer it takes to go through a phase, it seems."

I answer, "And I *am* getting older."

Ed counters, "But I think you are coming out of your most recent putting phase. That 66 you shot the first round in the du Maurier testifies that you had to make darned near everything you looked at. Yep, I think you're coming out of it."

"Boy, I hope. I really hope."

WHY DO MANY WOMEN BECOME DROPOUTS?

Many women are taking up golf these days because they think it might help them (1) lose weight, (2) gain friends, or (3) improve their business. Eighty-five percent of them will quit the game before they lose weight, gain friends, or improve their business.

Golf is not noted as a fat burner, but you probably will make new friends, and eventually, when you can play at an acceptable level, you might use golf as a business tool. But I personally believe golf should be an end in itself, not a lever to catapult you to success in another field.

The LPGA, in partnership with the Gillette Company, is sponsoring golf clinics around the country with the objective of getting women excited about golf.

Many women are taking up golf because they believe the game is a useful business tool. For decades men have been making deals on the golf course and at the nineteenth hole (the club bar). Business and professional women, not wanting to relinquish this asset, are now becoming interested in the game. Unfortunately, however, 85 percent of women beginners quit the game before they even start learning to play.
Photo by Betty Hicks

Joanne Winter, LPGA Teaching Professional of the Year in 1969 and winner of the Ellen Griffin Rolex award in 1995. The Ellen Griffin Rolex award was created to honor a professional, male or female, who has made a major contribution to the teaching of golf. Joanne, a pitching star for the Racine Belles in the All-American Girls Baseball League (as in *A League of Their Own*), advises players to remember their good shots and forget their bad ones. Joanne is important to me because she started the Arizona Silver Belle tournament for girls, which I underwrote for several years.

© Cheryl Traendly

Well, a lot of them get excited initially and then become dropouts. Why? I would have dropped out at age four if I could have, just because the game was so frustrating.

"Golf is not a natural game," Ed Jones reminds us.

I would add that women's priorities are not the same as men's. There are too many things that come first to them. Men's priorities, on the other hand, are sports—their leisure, their getaway, their release. Women have not really done that. So many men pros don't know how to relate to women students.

Why don't women golfers practice? Go to a driving range and count the number of women. Someone asked me, "Does the percentage of women out there practicing equal the percentage of women playing golf in America today?" No, of course it doesn't.

I answered, "Well, women golfers *are* taking more lessons. They're doing more practicing, but golf is a very time-consuming

WHY DO MANY WOMEN BECOME DROPOUTS?
continued

game. Women want to take a lesson and get instant results. So they'll hit a half a bucket of balls and then go play."

There are a lot of women who are not at all aggressive. They won't pick up a club and take command of the club. Says Ed, "The club takes command of them. Nothing could be more frustrating than trying to hit a golf ball when the club is swinging you and you're not swinging it."

You're the boss of that club. Don't let the club boss you!

Know that learning golf is a long-term process. I'm still learning, even though I am in the LPGA Hall of Fame. Do I get frustrated with the game? You bet I do! Perhaps that's part of its fascination. Bobby Jones once said, "You're seven years a beginner."

Know that you need to take lessons from a competent professional, preferably one who is a member of the LPGA Teaching and Club Professional Division. This organization really promotes improved golf instruction and screens its members carefully to assure they are good teachers. Don't get me wrong here. There are excellent men teachers. Ed Jones is a prime example. But you can be more assured that your instructor will be in tune with you, your limitations, and your motivation, if you choose an LPGA Teaching Professional.

You also need to have equipment that fits you—not just "ladies" clubs. I don't believe in giving golf clubs sexist labels. There are not "men's clubs" and "ladies clubs." There are simply clubs that fit you, no matter what your sex.

To golf, you must persist despite the frustration and the seeming lack of improvement. Try to find something joyful about each round of golf, about each practice session. Joanne Winter, an Arizona LPGA Teaching Professional, suggests, "Think about the good shots you hit today, not the bad ones."

INDEX